CW00971189

THE
WARS OF ROSIE

THE
WARS OF ROSIE

HARD KNOCKS, ENDURANCE, AND THE
'GEORGE DAVIS IS INNOCENT' CAMPAIGN

ROSE DEAN-DAVIS
AS TOLD TO PAUL WOODS

Pennant Books

First published in hardback 2009
by Pennant Books

Text copyright © 2008 by Rose Dean-Davis

The moral right of the author has been asserted.

All rights reserved. No part of this publication may be reproduced, stored in a retrieval system, or transmitted, in any form or by any means, electronic, mechanical, photocopying, recording or otherwise, without the prior permission in writing of the publisher, except by a reviewer who wishes to quote brief passages in connection with a review written for insertion in a newspaper, magazine or broadcast.

British Library Cataloguing-in-Publication Data:
A catalogue record for this book is available from
The British Library

ISBN 978-1-906015-32-9

Paul Woods wishes to express his gratitude to George Davis, Peter Chappell and Rick Davis for their kindness and generosity in agreeing to grant interviews for this book.

Design & Typeset by Envy Design Ltd

Printed in the UK by CPI William Clowes Beccles NR34 7TL

Pictures reproduced with kind permission of the author, from her personal archive, and with kind permission of Getty Images.

Every reasonable effort has been made to acknowledge the ownership of copyright material included in this book. Any errors that have inadvertently occurred will be corrected in subsequent editions provided notification is sent to the publisher.

Pennant Books
A division of Pennant Publishing Ltd
PO Box 5675
London W1A 3FB

www.pennantbooks.com

CONTENTS

DEDICATIONS

I'd like to dedicate this book to Peter, Colin, Jimmy, Richie and their wives. To Martin Walker, Ian Cameron and David Milner. To Bernadette, Geri and Bev. To all those people all over the country who supported me at the time of the campaign, including everyone up north. (The northerners are genuine people; they're how the East Enders used to be.)

I'd also like to thank Patsy and Pauline; Steven and his lovely wife Julie; his sister Elaine and her husband Rob; Danny and Lorraine. All of them are absolute diamonds, and I'd also like to mention their kids, who I've grown very close to: Jack, Sam and Grace; my dearest little friend Dulcie, who I loved looking after, and Casey, who's a little sweetheart.

To my dear friends Hetty, who has never missed a hospital appointment with me for nearly five years, and Maria, and their families. To my schoolfriend Jean – we've been friends since we were eleven and we still keep in touch. To my friends Alan and Stella, and their daughters. To Nicky, who I've known since she was a young girl.

ROSE DEAN-DAVIS

To Deana's friends, who have been so very, very good to me –
especially Denise.

I'm thankful for my four beautiful granddaughters,
my beautiful great granddaughter and my handsome
great grandson.

I hope there's no one I've forgotten, but those people who
are my friends know who I mean

Thank God that I've been able to find such decent friends.
This is the only way I can find to thank you for all that
you've done for me.

FOREWORD

I was asked many years ago to co-operate on a book about my life, and my role in the campaign to free George Davis, my ex-husband. I didn't think it was appropriate at the time, but now circumstances have changed. Now I see it as something to leave my family when I'm no longer here. Something to remember me by.

I always knew the campaign would go down in history – but the same wasn't necessarily true of my life story. I can only hope that I'll be remembered too.

We never knew at the time what the outcome would be, all we knew was that something had to be done. Every one of us on the campaign was different, everyone had a part to play and we all played it well.

I've never regretted it because I think it helped a lot of genuinely innocent people in prison, it encouraged them to take their cases to appeal and it helped to change the identification laws. It also taught me an awful lot – particularly about how to deal with the media.

And though I'd always been strong, it made me a stronger person. I see it in people when they talk to me now: *"Ooh, she's as hard as nails!"* I'm not hard. But if I'd been weak, where would I have been? Where would George have been? Where would the campaign have been?

I also had my kids to think about. No matter how low I felt at the time, I could never show them. Because a woman still has to get on with it and deal with all the mundane things – housework, shopping, going to work. Sometimes I've looked back and wondered how I coped with it all, but of course you just *do*.

Needs must when the devil drives.

You never know how your life is going to change. Being recognised during (and after) the campaign was never something I was proud of. In fact, I really didn't like it one bit. To find throngs of reporters outside your street door can make you go absolutely *mental*. The pressures of being in the public eye are intense – I can understand why these young pop stars go off the rails.

But it seemed that, once we were through it all, the way that George betrayed us afterwards just dismissed everything. It was as if a mist had suddenly cleared and there was nothing left in its place.

Life hasn't all been bad – far from it. I was fortunate to have good friends, and I've seen places that some people only dream of.

But it always seemed that as I got over one knock, something else would come along. And they were not things that you could just brush aside.

When my mother died she never left us any material possessions, but I believe that me and my brothers inherited our courage from her. So I'd really like to think that anyone on a down who reads this book will gain the strength to cope with whatever life throws at them. Because what I've had to contend with hasn't been easy. Thank God that I've come through it all – though I don't know about this time. But I never gave up. And even now, I will *never* give up.

Rosemary Dean, 2008

1

NUMBERS
AND OMENS

I was born at number thirteen, Kent Road, Chichester. My dad must have been stationed there during the war. It was beautiful.

My son took me back about four years ago, though I couldn't afford to live there now. It looks like a relatively new house, but I'm sixty-seven now so it's got to be over seventy years old. It's strange, because you look and you think, "It's not as big as I thought," because my mum had all these kids.

That number thirteen has carried me through a lot. It's not an unlucky number for me at all, though so many things have added up to seven too. Thirteen is six plus seven, and that seven has been prominent.

I got married on the seventh day of the sixth month. My first flat was number sixteen, and the one and the six in sixteen add up to seven.

I also lost two of my children on the seventh.

My dad's name was James Henry Dean. (My brother Jimmy, who died just before Christmas 2007, went on the telly for a programme about people named 'James Dean'.)

My mum's name was Rosetta Alice. My nan's name was Rose Barker, and I'm Rosemary.

My mum and dad were chalk and cheese, they really were complete opposites. My dad was a very law-abiding citizen – the law was the law. He was a typical army man. I don't think he was quite sixteen when he joined, although he made out that he was. He was in the regular army for twenty-four years, so he was very disciplined. If you walked around with no shoes on he used to hit the roof, and he had a thing about cleaning his shoes.

My mum, on the other hand, was a fiddler who ducked and dived. She had to, just to fetch us all up. I thought a lot of my dad in my own way, but when I look back I can see my mum had a terribly hard life. But I never really heard her complain; in fact, I think it all kept her going.

She had terribly bad legs, with thrombosis phlebitis from as far back as I can remember. It was from having a big family. She'd cook all day but she couldn't kneel to do housework, so we were all taught to do it – even my brothers. My brother Alan could scrub a house out at fourteen better than any woman. We all had our bits to do. Even when I was at work, I still couldn't go out until I'd washed up and tidied the kitchen. It was expected, but if you ask the kids today they look at you like you're mad, don't they?

Now my mum had been married twice, but I only learnt this as I got older. She had two boys, my two eldest brothers, and she was going through a divorce when my dad, who she already knew, came back after seven years in India. I don't suppose it was a secret, but my mum lived with my dad before they got married while my nan brought my two eldest brothers up.

With me being the youngest girl, brought up with my four

other brothers, I had to be that little bit tougher. I think my eldest brother, Richard, was sixteen or seventeen when my mum had me. My next eldest brother was Kenny, he must have been fourteen as there's not two years between them. Then came my sisters, Doreen and Brenda. My Doreen was my dad's first one by my mum – she's dead now, God rest her soul. Doreen was about nine when I was born, Brenda was eight, so there wasn't quite a year between them. Then came Alan, who must have been about six, and then there was Colin, who we've just buried.[1] There must have been four years between me and him. Then there was Jimmy, me and David, my younger brother.

All my mum's kids were blond, except Colin and me who were the only two dark ones. The others were as white as my dad was, whereas my mum was dark. I can't remember a time when we weren't close as kids, but as we all got older we drifted apart. I've got one brother and one sister left now out of nine of us.

When my mum and dad came back to London, my earliest memory is of living next door to my nan in a great big tenement house. I was four. We lived in Stockmar Road, just off Morning Lane, Hackney.

There was another family who lived upstairs and we had the next floor down, a great big area. I can remember going to the nursery at the back of the Hackney Empire, my older brother used to take me and David. In those days they used to have the trolley buses, they used to go round by a pub which is still there in Sylvester Road.

I remember VE Day. My dad made the cake for the street party and I sat on the wall outside. Everyone was excited,

---

1 *In April 2008.*

happy and singing, all the women had their aprons on. Of course, food was rationed then, so everyone made something for the street party. We had jelly, though Christ knows where they got it from! It was an exciting day, the first party I ever went to.

My dad was in his army uniform and there were a lot of soldiers on leave. I think he was stationed in Chelsea Barracks. He wasn't a very amiable man, but everyone was jolly and had beer or whatever. I think my dad was on the verge of being demobbed. He was a cook in the Royal Artillery, and I imagine my mum probably said, "It would be nice if you made the cake." He was a good cook, both of them were. My mum could make a meal out of anything, and it was proper food.

From there we moved to Retreat Place. It was an old house, a nice house, very similar to the one I'm living in now, with a little backyard and a back gate. Every Saturday afternoon was a ritual. My mum would put the copper kettle on and fill the tin bath out in the yard. I was always the first one in, so I was the lucky one. Whoever got in last had all the dirt from the others. She'd wash your hair under the cold tap and pour vinegar water over it: "That keeps lice and fleas away!"

We hadn't lived there long when I started school. I went to Isabella Road School in Homerton. They were happy times and, being one of the youngest, I was more fortunate than the older ones really. We didn't have a lot, but when you're a kid you don't ask where things come from, like clothes. If you were told to put them on, you put them on – whether they came from a second-hand shop, the rag shop or whatever.

My granddaughters have asked me, "Oh Nan, did you wear second-hand clothes?" I said, "Yeah, I was brought up

4

in second-hand clothes." There's no shame in that. Everybody, not only our family, had nothing.

In those days you had tally men,[2] so at Easter time, holiday time, we always had new clothes. But we could only wear them over the holidays. Then they'd go to the pawnshop. You never asked questions, you didn't say, "Where's my clothes?" You just took it for granted that you'd probably not see them anymore. My mum would take them to the pawnshop and then she'd sell the ticket.

You couldn't do it now, could you? Can you imagine it, with the kids in their designer clothes? My mum would go down the Lane[3] on a Sunday and come back with shoes if she thought they'd fit. If they didn't, I'd squeeze my foot in if I liked them. Or if they were too big you'd be frightened to skip, in case you came out of them.

But I was never ashamed. Even now I love going in charity shops, just to support them. I have a clearout now and again, and take it to the hospice for their jumble sales. I was 'Second-hand Rose', but I always say to my kids, "Try and buy the best because it's better in the long run." If you can afford the best, have the best, because I've always had everybody else's leftovers.

My brother used to say he was the only kid in his class who could take his trousers off without undoing the buttons. My younger brother David came in one day, crying. My mum went, "What are you crying for?"

---

2 *The tally man was a familiar figure in pre-war, wartime and post-war London, and other British cities. Basically a salesman who sold goods 'on tick', his instalment terms made day-to-day existence more liveable for the cash-strapped working class.*
3 *'The Lane' is derived from Petticoat Lane, its name up until the early nineteenth century; long since renamed as Middlesex Street, London E1.*

"All the kids have got football boots!" he said.

She went down the Lane and said, "I've got you a nice pair."

He was only out five minutes, then he came back crying again. "The kids said they ain't football boots!"

They weren't. They were girl's boots with a zip up the front. But they were leather, so my mum thought he could kick the ball with them.

My mum earned a living out of second-hand clothes. She was a forager, a really strong person, and she instilled that into us.

My mum knew what she was looking for. She'd buy Ming vases, and she knew they were worth a few bob. Or she'd buy silver; she always used to say, "Look for the lion."[4] She was like an antique dealer really, though she dealt more in clothes. My old nan used to come down the Lane with us sometimes. Whereas my mum was rough and ready, my nan was such a smart lady that she'd never go out without her hat and her little gloves on. She always looked immaculate, with little brown lace-up heeled shoes.

My mum had this pair of Ming vases, she gave one to my nan and one to me to hold, while she put all her bits in a big black sack. We got on at Bromley-by-Bow station and my mum said to my nan, "Hold that a minute, Mum." My nan was putting her gloves on, and she only went and broke the vase! One was no good; you were only okay if you had the pair.

Even now, going to Bart's,[5] I get a lump in my throat when I look over at Smithfield Market. Every Christmas Eve, my mum and me – or if it wasn't me it would be my

---

4 For centuries 'The Lion Passant' (in walking position) was the recognised hallmark for British silver, and still is in London, Birmingham and Sheffield.

5 St Bartholomew's Hospital.

older brother, or the younger one – would get her pushchair and line up really early in the morning, the earliest we could get there.

She'd get turkeys for, say, five or six neighbours, and put a couple of bob on each. That helped pay for ours and a leg of pork. (As funny as my dad was, he'd cook all day on Christmas Eve. He'd make cakes and cook a turkey or a goose.)

For hours we used to stand outside; it was freezing cold in the fog and the smog, she'd wrap a big scarf around us.

And often now, when I look over there, I think I can see my mum standing there with the pushchair. She wouldn't let anyone push in. *Oh no.* She'd give them what for.

My mum was a true East Ender. She didn't give a shit! My mum gave it to you so straight that she was embarrassing. But she never suffered with depression, because whatever she had to say came out. That's why half the girls today are depressed, because they can't speak out, they hold everything back.

My mum always used to say, if you've got a friend you should be able to say what you think without them taking offence. If you get it off your mind, you're not worrying about it. The old girls years ago didn't have time to be depressed. Now they've got counsellors for it.

When we were living at Retreat Place, my dad came home and told us we were going out for the day. They'd got a coach for all the kids to go to Clacton. I think they paid about a shilling a week for all us kids. Oh how we looked forward to that, for weeks and weeks!

As you got on the coach, I can remember them pinning a badge on with a bit of rag. (I suppose that was to blow your nose with.) We were each given a little bag with something to eat in it. We had a lovely, lovely day, and spoke about it for weeks after because we never went to the seaside. It was the first time I'd ever seen sea and sand. I couldn't have been any older than six. We never had holidays, not even when we were older really – though I went away with my nan a few times.

If you heard there was a works beano, all the men would have a drink before they set off to wherever they were going for the day. As a kid, you'd turn up early at the pub. As they got on the coach they used to throw all their odd pennies and coppers, and you'd run around picking them up. (They do that in Ireland too, at weddings.)

And then we were moving. Our house came under compulsory purchase order, so we were the first tenants at number one Cannock House, Woodbury Downs, at Stamford Hill. I must have been six when we moved there. It was a very modern flat in those days, with four bedrooms. In one of the bedrooms there was even a fitted dressing table – I couldn't get over it: *"Ooh look!"* – and a chest of drawers.

We used to go to the Saturday morning pictures at Stamford Hill. Coming home after the films, you'd get the Jewish ladies, or their men, standing at their gates asking you to light their fire. They would give you a biscuit or a sweet, which we used to look forward to, though I didn't understand the religious side of it. You wouldn't let a kid go in anyone's house now, would you? But we used to go in and light their candles.

And then my eldest brother moved to Debden. It wasn't long after the war really. My mum had gone down there to see him, and I can remember her coming back, saying to my dad, "Oh, it's lovely down there."

We only lived at Woodbury Downs for about eighteen months before my mum got a house in Debden. She said it would do us kids good, so we moved. I wasn't quite eight then. We had a great big house – at least to a kid. Of course, I've been back since and what I thought was enormous is just ordinary. But because we were at the end house, we had the biggest garden with mains going through for the water pipes.

I have happy memories of Debden.[6] Even though it was hard for my mum, we had a happy childhood. My brothers might not have agreed, but I look back on it with fondness. It was all new property, all new houses, and it was like the countryside to a kid.

When we first went there there were no shops, no schools. You had one bus that went into Loughton. Your nearest shop, a little paper shop, was in Borders Lane about a mile away. They used to send double-decker buses – my mum got a job on one, looking after the kids – and we used to go to Chingford for school, in tin Nissan huts which the army must have had during the war. They made them into classrooms, and they were absolutely freezing. You had to wear your coat in school during the winter.

And then, when the holidays came, the summers were absolutely beautiful. We'd never seen so much grass, or horses in the fields. At the side of the road, when you walked down country lanes, *"Oh, what's that?"* You'd touch it and it would move. I'd never seen a hedgehog in my life before. You'd get jam jars with bits of string and go newt fishing in the streams.

You'd see rabbits – which we had seen, because my mum used to keep rabbits and chickens, but not *wild* rabbits. We

---

6 *Debden was built as an Essex 'new town' by the London County Council between 1947 and 1952, initially to re-house people whose homes were damaged during the war. It is now part of the Epping Forest district suburbs to the far east of London.*

used to go blackberry picking, pea picking, potato picking, tomato picking, in the school holidays. That was another way of my mum earning a few bob. The more you picked, the more money you got. We used to get on the back of a lorry, they'd pick you up at a certain time to take you down to Kent, but we didn't feel we were helping our mum really. It was an adventure.

My old dad loved hop picking because it was out in the open. He cooked on the open fire. We were only there three, four, maybe five days, but my mum *hated* it while my dad didn't want to come home.

Not that we had a lot, but my mum wasn't used to roughing it. The beds were made of straw, you had take all your own bedding, they weren't nice, soft mattresses, but we had featherbeds at home.

Twice a week a lorry used to come round because we never had any shops, to sell sugar or tea. There was nothing where we lived, only beautiful houses. It was mainly East Enders that had moved down there after the war. I've been back a few times since, there are still a lot of the old neighbours living there, but it's sad to go back now.

In the holidays we'd walk for miles, from Debden to Grange Farm at Chingford. There was an open-air swimming pool there. My mum would make us a big bag of sandwiches, with powdered lemonade in milk bottles, and we'd be gone all day long. Give us all a towel each and we made our own entertainment.

I can remember the lady across the road, Mrs Fitz, when we hadn't lived at Debden long. She'd got married late in life and had this little boy, who was about four. John, her husband, came running over to my mum one Sunday morning, hysterical.

He said, "I think she's had a heart attack! Can you get an ambulance?" We didn't have phones then, but one of the neighbours did and called for an ambulance. My mum went with him, but his wife died. She was a lovely lady.

The day of the funeral was during school holiday time. We all watched the funeral; I watched the people's faces, how they were crying, how they were all pulling funny expressions. And I laughed. My mum didn't half hit me when she came back from the funeral, but it was my nerves that did it.

I don't know how old I was when the first school was built at Debden. They used to teach us how to dance with the bells there, like Morris dancers. But my dad was ill all the time we lived there.

He had emphysema and the sap in the trees didn't agree with him. He'd been the first European to be given a certain form of quinine for malaria in India, which had been caused by gnats, so that may have had something to do with it.

Still, he made an allotment in the garden, planted potatoes and runner beans. (Talk about 'the good life'! It really was, because it was all organic.)

But it was hard for my mum, it really was a struggle. We never had family allowance then. I don't think that came into play until I was about eleven. Of course, my mum and dad were staunch Labour voters.

But you couldn't pick a newspaper up. My dad would go mad. "Put that paper down!" You used to think, "Why? I want to read it." Of course, it was a way of protecting you as to what was going on in the world. They didn't think it was educating you; they didn't want you to know that there were wars, they didn't want you to know what was happening in the Far East.

My mum would swear, though I very rarely heard my dad swear. When I got older, I asked her, "Mum, why do you swear a lot?" She'd say, "To stop me fucking hitting all of you's!" She was a proper Ada Larkin.

She'd be f-ing and blinding and my dad used to go, "Tut-tut-tut! Go and wash your mouth out." Well, you can imagine what she said to him! You would never have put my mum and dad together; at least I wouldn't have. My dad was a relatively quiet man, a very miserable man. But then as a kid you don't understand – he was ill. I used to think he was lazy, though he did work for two years as the caretaker of a girls' private school, when we lived in Debden. There's a lovely photo of my dad, all of the girls and the headmistress. It wasn't a hard job, it was just blackening the blackboards and keeping the general grounds tidy. He couldn't do a heavy job.

But on a Saturday morning I'd say to him, "Can I come with you, Dad?"

"Yeah, you can empty all the baskets."

So I went there with him, and in one basket was a little porcelain figurine with a piece of the hand missing.

"They're throwing this, can I have it Dad?"

He said that, as long as it was in the basket, it meant it was going to be thrown out. But I didn't have it long. I took it home. My mum washed it. She knew it was chipped, but she knew she could get a few bob for it. So it went.

She was clever, my mum, she had an eye for things. (As did my two elder brothers. Colin, who died recently, was a proper hoarder.) It helped to bring us all up. She worked bloody hard, and she had a hard life.

My dad bred Alsatians, that was his hobby. I used to say, "I'm sure Daddy likes the dogs more than he likes us." I can never remember him even giving me a peck on the cheek.

We'd had the dog mated and they'd had pups, like little balls of fluff. Where my mum used to buy and sell second-hand clothes, she might have bonnets or little booties. We'd put the bonnets on the pups and we'd be laughing because they'd be running around with them on. But as soon as my dad came in, that laughter had to stop.

He had a soft side to him, but we didn't see it very often. I used to say to my mum, "I don't know how you had all us kids," he was so miserable.

I think my mum took the world on. I'm not saying my dad didn't worry, but when she got over one meal she must have been worrying about what she was going to give us tomorrow. For breakfast, my mum had big, crusty loaves that she cut into chunks with milk and sugar. My grandchildren go, "Oh Nan, you had *that*?" We used to love it, it was a porridge. I can never remember coming home from school and my mum not being there. She always had something on the cooker.

We weren't allowed to talk at the table. My dad would go, "Get on with your food!" but we'd say, "What we got for afters?" My mum used to say, "It's enough getting the fucking befores!" But we always had afters, whether it was a big lump of bread pudding or jelly and blancmange. She was a good grubber, we always had good food.

Looking back, now I'm older and wiser, I think, "How did my mum do it? How did my mum cope?" But then I sometimes think, "How have *I* coped?" But you do, don't you? Somehow you get through whatever life throws at you. Then, when you do cope, people think you're hard. But you have to get that bit tougher, otherwise you would sink.

When we lived in Debden we used to go to jumble sales on a Saturday. My mum would get the local paper and we'd go to Woodford, or Epping. We'd always get there early and

13

we'd look through the window. My mum said to me one day, "See them shoes, get them – don't matter what they're like, get them!"

And she gave me a pound, which was a lot of money then. As soon as the doors opened, I've gone over to the shoes and put them in this black bag. Coming back on the train, my mum's got this basket and I'm delving through it. Inside was a compact; when I opened it, it was a solid gold bracelet. It was what they called a lover's knot bracelet with a little card: "To my darling wife on our anniversary."

I went, "Oh, ain't that lovely?"

"Now give that 'ere, that's not to be played with!"

I knew where that was going. She sorted out the shoes and half of them had got holes. "You'd buy anything!" she said.

"But you *told me* to buy them!"

She passed the buck to me, but she must have got a nice few bob for that bracelet.

I had a little friend who I used to go home with from school occasionally, and she was an only child. She had a beautiful bedroom and she seemed to have everything, like a little sewing machine. So I said, "I'm going to get a sewing machine for Christmas."

Yeah, I did get one. As I ripped the paper open I thought, "The box is all bent." My mum had bought it at a jumble sale. It was rusty, the needle was broken.

"Oh gawd blimey, she's broke it already. She ain't had it five minutes!"

It was years later that my mum said, "I bought that with the needle broke." You just wouldn't do it to a kid today. But she tried her best. We never went short of food, which was the most important thing.

When we moved to Debden, my second eldest sister,

Brenda, who was eight years older than me, must have been sixteen, and the older one, Doreen, was seventeen. I know we hadn't lived there long before Brenda applied for a job waitressing on the Isle of Wight; I can remember her going away.

I don't know where Doreen met her husband, but he was a sailor, as was my other sister's husband. I can see them walking down towards our house in their uniforms, so smart and handsome, their white caps stuck on the back of their heads, and their white tabards.

Doreen's bloke – they weren't married then – said, "I'm going to make you a doll's house." I never had a lot of toys. My mum would go down the Lane on Sunday mornings, but just to buy bits and bobs: "That will fit him, this will fit her." Whatever didn't fit us, she washed, pressed and sold to the neighbours, which was how she earned a few bob.

So every time my sister's fellah was home on leave, he'd make a bit more of this doll's house. It was kept in the corner of the front room with a blanket over it. He would say to me, "If you cheat and look at it, I won't give it to you." So I never, ever did.

The day finally came when he gave it to me; I must have been ten. It was a beautiful doll's house. He'd made furniture – I can see him now with tweezers, putting the screws in the wardrobe. The big, old, round electric switches were on the side, with little tiny bulbs inside. Oh, I thought it was wonderful!

I couldn't wait to tell the kids in school. I used to run home from school to play with it. Then, after two weeks, I came home and found it wasn't there. I went, "Mum, where's my doll's house?" She said, "The dog chewed the roof, I've had to take it to the doll's hospital." Every day I came home, I used to ask, "Is it done yet, is it ready?" In the end I just gave up.

Many years later, I asked my mum what happened to that doll's house. She said, "I owed a month's rent, girl, and I had to sell it. It was either that or we were going to be chucked out."

So to compensate for the doll's house – she hadn't told me at that stage that she'd sold it, I was still a little girl – she bought me a big rag doll. It was like a little teenager really, stuffed with straw. I came home one day from school and the dog had chewed half of one leg off, all the straw was hanging out. Of course, I started crying.

My dad said, "What's the matter with you?" I said, "Look what the dog's done to my doll!" It was one of his amiable days. He went, "Give it here." Next thing, he'd got a pair of scissors and cut the other leg off. I started crying again. *"What have you done?"* He said, "Look, when it's got its long frock on you won't know it's got no legs." He'd levelled them off. I can laugh about it now, but back then . . .

My oldest sister married the man who made me the doll's house. He came from Margate, a very quiet, lovely man. He only died about four years ago. I never heard that man once raise his voice. Doreen died about ten years ago, and he never got over it. If ever a couple were happy, it was them.

By the time we'd moved to Debden, my two eldest brothers had already got married. There were all those years between us. After my sisters had gone, I was the only girl left with four brothers. I was the youngest but one.

In 1952, when I was eleven, it was the Queen's Coronation and we had the street party there. They were happy days. But my dad was quite ill and my mum was trying to get back to London.

Churchill was still the Prime Minister then, and my mum

wrote to him. That was the difference between my mum and dad. My dad could read and write, he wasn't illiterate, but my mum passed matriculation[7] in her day. "My husband did twenty-four years in the army for this country . . ." She went on to say that she wanted to come back because of my dad's ill health, and no one was doing anything about it. She could really put a letter together, always finishing it: "Anticipating an early reply." *Get on with it, I want a reply!* She got her reply, I think it was just a standard letter. But it had the stamp '10 Downing Street', so my mum couldn't get over it.

She was very educated, her English put mine to shame. And yet my mother never instilled that in us. She was one of five children, and my nan was left on her own at thirty-four. So my mum had to pack up school and go out to work in a box-making factory, she couldn't go on to further education. I think she resented the fact that she had four younger siblings she had to help bring up, and that's why they all lost touch. They only seemed to meet up after my nan died.

Whether my mum thought her education was wasted and ours would be the same, I don't know. But she never encouraged any of us. My sister who's still alive has done numerous office jobs. Yet the rest of us were good with our hands.

My mum went here, there and everywhere to try to get us back to London. By this time my sisters were married and I was the only girl at home, with four brothers. So, to make it even worse, she said in the letter that I'd had to go and live with my nan in Hackney, because she only had so many bedrooms.

---

7 *Prior to the introduction of the General Certificate of Education (GCE) in British schools, the matriculation exam was the standard entry test before a pupil could go on to higher education.*

Now that the boys were getting older and I was eleven, it wasn't right that I should have to sleep in the same room.

So I had to live with my nan from Monday to Friday and go home at weekends. My mum had put this in the letter. And of course they could verify it, because I had to leave school at Debden to come to Hackney, so they couldn't say that my mum was telling porky pies.

It was lovely going back at weekends from Hackney to Debden. There was no comparison, I missed it all. Near where we lived there was a field where shire horses grazed, with big hooves. We called one of the horses 'Dolly' and named it 'Dolly's Field'. It stuck, it's still called Dolly's Field today. We used to spend hours over there with the horses.

But I was sent to the Hackney Free and Parochial School. My nan was still living in Stockmar Road, next door to the house that we lived in before we moved to Retreat Place. She was a housekeeper for two court dressmakers. It was a great big tenement house and she had the room right at the very top, and the kitchen and scullery downstairs. Mick and Doll, the dressmakers, had the rest of the house.

The family allowance must have been around by now, because my mum was supposed to give my nan eight shillings, which is equivalent to 40p. She got it on a Monday, but she never gave it to her because she'd spend it. She'd say, "Tell Nanny I'll be down Wednesday." I'd walk into my nan's kitchen on a Monday morning and they'd be having their breakfast, because she used to cook their meals. And my nan would say, "Has your mother sent me anything?"

I'd go, "No, but Mum will be down Wednesday, Nan."

"I don't know how your mother thinks I can keep you for nothing!"

That is the first time I ever felt humiliated. I wouldn't have taken any notice if they hadn't have been there, but they were all eating. I felt terrible, but I never said anything. I wouldn't ever be rude to my nan.

She had a hard life too. She had next to nothing, but what she had she cherished. There was a leather armchair that you could see your face in, it was spotless. She had a big jar in her kitchen. She used to keep the tea from the teapot, put it in the jar with salt and then, every morning, get a handful and throw it on the carpet, all over the floor, and sweep it. That's an old-fashioned thing. The tealeaves and salt saved the dust from coming up. She'd pick the carpet up, take it out in the yard, shake it, turn it face up on the grass, and it used to fetch all the colours out in the mat.

She had the old fashioned fire range. She used to Black Lead[8] it, and you could see your face in that too. We never had television then, we had the radio, so she'd say, "There's a good play on tonight. I'll get done here and then we'll sit and listen to it." She wasn't a smoker, but she used to have one fag and that was her treat every night.

She never, ever spoke about my granddad – he died very young – but she always had this plaster on her wrist. I used to ask, "Nan, your arm's been bad for a long while. What's going on?"

"Mind your own business, Nose Ointment."

She had her husband's initials, and she was ashamed of it. I see the kids today with tattoos, and my dad was covered in them, smothered in snakes and naked ladies on his chest and back. But it must have been going back to the late nineteenth century when my nan had it done. (My mum was born in

8 *Grate polish.*

1905.) It wasn't until I got older that she let me see it. It was very tiny, but it was a tattoo.

They still had their Victorian ways though. My nan's sister came in one day when my mum must have been about fourteen, and said, "I've just seen your Rosie up the street having a crossbar on a bike, showing all her ankles" – her *ankles*! What would they think about today?

My mum was like the black sheep of the family. My nan had four daughters and one son – my Uncle Dick, who was the second eldest after my mum. He was the deputy manager of Dunstable Motorworks, the image of Clark Gable, with jet-black, wavy hair and a little black 'tache. My nan would take me to Uncle Dick and Aunt Lillie's for a holiday, and that was the first time I ever saw a table napkin. They were really posh.

Now he'd been born and bred in the East End, but he was educated. He'd learned quickly and he wanted a better way of life, though I never heard him speak posh. My Aunt Lillie was lovely. They had two daughters, Janet and Valerie, one was a year older than me and one a year younger. She used to send me all their cast-offs; Mum used to like their dresses.

When we went there, it was the first time I ever saw French doors leading out into a garden. My nan said, "Watch your manners, do what everyone else does." My mum did teach us our manners, but a table napkin – what's that? "Put it down your front!"

I often wondered how my mum would have finished up if her father had lived. She could probably have gone a long way. Her youngest sister, Aunt Ann, had married a science master at Oxford.

My Aunt May and Aunt Esther were true East Enders, but my Aunt Ann used to see my nan once a year. She used to fetch her a dozen eggs and give her a £5 note. One year I came home from somewhere, I don't know where, and my nan was sitting at the table crying.

"What are you crying for, Nan?"

"Nothing, nothing!"

When my mum came down I could hear them talking. (You know what you're like when you're a kid, earwigging.) My nan had written to my Aunt Ann, said it was lovely seeing her and whatever, thanking her for the money. And Aunt Ann had written back, saying, "Mum, please don't write to me at the college because your handwriting's terrible."

Oh, my mum went *mental*, I could hear her shouting. My nan had worked bloody hard to bring them up and she'd turned them into snobs. But whereas she'd had a hard life, she did encourage them to make better lives for themselves. I only ever met my Aunt Ann once, and that was at my nan's funeral.

"I don't know where I got your mother from," she used to say to me. But my nan stuck by my mum because she had all the kids.

When there was nothing on the radio, I'd sit and ask my nan questions. If she didn't want to answer, then she wouldn't answer. But if I got her talking about when she lost her husband, and how all she had was her widow's pension, she'd tell me she used to lay out and wash the dead.

"Oh, you washed *dead* people?"

"There were some people died with their eyes open, so you had to close their eyelids, put pennies on them; tie their jaws up; stuff their mouth with cotton wool." You couldn't tell a kid about that now, but I was inquisitive.

Little did I know that I would use everything she told me in later life. It's like she could see into the future.

She said, "I used to get half a crown for doing that, you

know," and it helped her to buy food or whatever. The girls today don't know how lucky they are, do they? They never got the handouts then. It was one and six to call the doctor out.

I was living with my nan for two years, and was very close to her. I can remember her saying to me, "See how nice you can do the scullery" – the old sculleries were all drab – "and make sure the corner's clean." She was a good teacher.

But she died of breast cancer, and in those days they couldn't do anything for you. She was very close to my oldest brother, Richard, and went to live with him; she actually died in his house just off Devons Road, which is at Bromley-by-Bow. He'd moved back from Debden when the prefabs first came out, the mobile home-type things.

I was sixteen when my nan died. She was a lovely lady. She was only little, but she was feisty, though not as feisty as my mum.

When my mum did get back to London, she came to number three Corbyn House, a three-bedroom place at Devons Road. When they moved into Corbyn House I came back. I was about thirteen.

Then I started school at Roman Road. But I'd developed a habit then that, looking back now, I realise was something I used to do all the time.

When were back at Debden, as my brother had a baby by then, my mum used to mind him when his wife went to work. He was about eight or nine months old. I'd gone into the front room, he was in his pram. He'd just woken up, he was all excited, and I took him out of his harness. But because he was so excited, I dropped him on the concrete floor! My dad went berserk. The nearest hospital was St Margaret's, in Epping, and nobody had phones. He had a fractured skull. My brothers used to say after that, "Ol'

Drop-the-baby, Ol' Drop-the-baby!" and of course they made me a bundle of nerves.

My mum used to say, "If I see you put your fucking hand in your mouth and touch your hair, I'm going to take you somewhere." It was nerves.

Anyway, once the school noticed it, she said, "I'm going to take you to see a psychiatrist."

"What's a psychiatrist?"

"A mental doctor!" my brothers used to say.

It was a great big office. The doctor said to my mum, "Go and sit in that corner." The doctor was sitting at this big desk. She got a bit of paper, told me to hold it and cut out a window.

She said to me, "If I opened that, what would it be?"

I'd said it'd be a square, which it would. So she got another bit of paper and cut out a half-moon.

"If I opened that, what would it be?"

I said it would be a circle. She said to my mum, "There's nothing wrong with this child. Who sent you here?"

It was weird, but I stopped doing the thing with my hand and my hair. But the school said I needed to go away on convalescence, because of my nerves.

So they sent me to this place called Warnham Court, at Horsham in Sussex. It was like a big stately home for children who had come from broken homes, or whose parents couldn't cope with them. My mum had just moved into Corbyn House while I was there. I actually went back there a couple of years ago to take some photos.

When I told my granddaughters all this, they sat and cried. I went, "Oh, don't fucking *cry!* What you crying for?"

"Oh Nan, isn't it sad?"

"But it's the truth!"

It was actually the most beautiful place. They had tennis

courts there, a great big posh house. It seemed like *Alice in Wonderland*. I was there for three months. They had a big tuck shop in the main hall where you kept all your sweets. That was open once a day, and you were allowed to take out all the sweets you wanted. One of the lady teachers was the sister of Ronald Shiner, the film star. And once a month, your parents could come down and visit you.

When I'd been there about three weeks, the next week was when the visits were due. But my mum couldn't afford to. There was a girl from the same flats as us who was also there, so my mum sent a parcel along with her mum for me. All the parents came down, and there was only me and a couple of other kids who didn't have their mum and dad there. So to make up for it, Mr Shaw, the headmaster, and his wife used to take us in the office and read us stories. I was twelve then, and I had my thirteenth birthday at Warnham House.

I accepted it. I think I was used to it by then, so I didn't feel left out. My mum did come down eventually, and she said how lovely it was. And while I was there, the Festival of Britain was coming up at County Hall. Mr Shaw said to me, "I'd like to give you a test."

I said, "What sort of test?" (I've always been a bit cheeky.)

"I want to give you a newsreel test." It was to find out whether I could entertain an audience. He said he was going to do it on cine-camera. He and his wife gave me a script, and I sat there and read it.

"What is it, a play?"

"No, it's poetry. Now I want you to read it, but I want you to *act* it too."

Well I must have done well, they both clapped.

"We're looking for someone to represent the school,"

he said, "but you'd have to get up on a stage and talk to an audience."

"Mm, I don't fancy doing that."

"I think you do," he said. And in fact I did.

They've got that on cine-film: me at County Hall for a week, standing up in front of so many hundreds of people and explaining what the school was about, what we did there in the dormitories and the dining hall. I won a prize for that, and they must still have it in the archives.

I loved those three months at Warnham Court. I won three prizes, one for a show and one for making a stool. I had to sing, "My grandfather's clock was too large for the shelf, so it stood ninety years on the floor . . ." I'll never forget that. I won two book vouchers – the first book I ever bought was *Little Women*, the first book I ever read.

I didn't resent it, and I think you accept things more as a kid. When I was little they'd go, "Hands up those having free dinners," and everyone would put their hand up. But as times got better my dad wasn't getting any better, and my mum wasn't getting any more money. It seemed it was only us putting our hands up. Then you started feeling like you were being singled out. You wouldn't do it to a kid today.

When I was fourteen we moved from Corbyn House to a big four-bedroom place at Brimsdown House, in Bromley-by-Bow. Underneath us were Mrs Raj and her husband, who were Indian. They were a nice family. Her boy came up to us one day: "Mum said could you spare two bits of bread, and would you mind buttering it?"

So I said, "What do you think this is, the Co-op?"

My mum went *wallop!* "Don't you ever let me hear you say that!" I had a great big lip come up.

Because then, people *did* help one another. My mum

couldn't abide laziness, but if you were ill my mum was there. My mum would nurse you all day. She'd help anybody.

I only had a year to go at school then. I'd made friends with a girl called Jean – her single name was Davis, funnily enough – and we're still friends today. Her brother was the youngest European featherweight boxer. Jim Wicks, the boxing promoter, took Bill Davis on. Bill fought Terry Spinks; Spinks won at the Empire Pool, Wembley; then they had a return fight and Billy beat him. My daughter would later be his bridesmaid.

(They're a lovely family. Jean's kids are friends with my son, and she and I have been friends since school. We don't see one another very often, but she phones occasionally and we keep in touch with birthday cards and Christmas cards. But she's there if you need her, the same as I would be for her.)

Back in the fifties we still had all our traditions. They're going now, which I find hard to accept. I'm not a religious person, far from it, but you never hear church bells, do you? When we were kids the bells told you it was Sunday. At Christmas you'd have the Salvation Army coming round the street, they'd send someone and you'd put a little something in an envelope. That's gone.

Alright, you can't send kids carol singing now unless they've got an adult with them. But we loved it. I'm sure my brother used to nick half of the money. I'd say, "How much we get off that old girl?"

"Oh, she only give us tuppence." She probably gave him two bob.[9] But we loved going out carol singing. The kids today are missing out, I think, with technology as it now is.

---

9 *Two bob = two shillings under the old l, s & d (pounds, shillings and pence) system, or 10p in decimal currency.*

(I look at my son's kids – they're on the computers, they're never out playing.)

I wanted to work with kids, I suppose because I'd always had little ones around me like my nieces and nephews. There used to be a place called Langley House along East India Dock Road. As I went by there on the bus you'd see the kids sitting on the windowsill, looking out, and they'd wave. I used to wave back.

"Poor little sods!" I said to my mum. "I'd love to get a job in there."

She went, "Well, go and knock and ask!"

So I went in to see the matron, or whoever was in charge.

"Have you got any positions?"

"Have you got any qualifications?"

"Oh. No."

"Well, I'm afraid you wouldn't be able to work here."

So I said, "Surely you don't need qualifications to be kind?" Which is true, isn't it?

But I had no chance of working there. So I went home and my mum said, "I've got you a job. You're starting at the Sussex Laundry on Monday."

I worked alongside Lizzie, she was a really nice lady who showed me how to do things. I used to feed her machine. I'd do my work, but she couldn't do hers until I'd done mine.

I'd been there about six weeks, and I didn't know it was rude to ask someone how much they earned. (You don't at that age, do you? I know it now!) And they don't always tell you the truth anyway.

Lizzie was like a mother figure. But I had a full card, and I was getting two pounds, seventeen shillings and sixpence a week.

I said, "We don't get a lot of money here, do we? It's quite hard work. How much do you get, Liz?"

"I get six pounds, ten shillings a week," she said.

"Well that ain't fair! I'm doing the same work as you and I'm keeping up with you. If I wasn't doing my work you wouldn't be able to do yours." I didn't even think about age – she was a married woman with kids; I'd just left school.

I didn't know that you had to go to the forelady if you had a grievance. So on my lunchtime, I went over her and knocked on Mr Turner the manager's door.

"Come in." I walked in.

"How can I help?"

"Mr Turner, could you explain something to me?"

"If I can."

"Can you tell me why Lizzie gets . . . And I only get . . . ?"

He looked at me with his mouth open, and he said, "I tell you what. I'm going to give you a rise for your cheek."

And I was put up to six pounds and ten shillings. That was a lot of money then. Of course, the forelady found out and went apeshit. "You must never, *ever* do it!" she said.

"Well, I didn't know. But I didn't think it was right." I wasn't told the ins and outs, the politics, of how the factory was run.

It was a hard lesson, but it did me a favour because it got me a rise. My mother couldn't believe it, she was over the moon. But then if I don't think something's fair I've always said so.

By this time I'd already met George, when I was fourteen and a half. He was two months younger than me. When I was still at school you'd have your tea and couldn't go out until you'd washed up and done your chores. And then I'd go round to my friend Jean's, where her mum always made me welcome. I used to love going round there because they were all so close, it was lovely to see.

Around the corner they had an off licence and all the kids used to sit on the wall, all the boys and girls used to mix. That's how I met George, after they'd just buried his nan. Then we used to see one another on the school bus. He went to Coopers College, which used to be at Mile End then, because he'd passed the scholarship. He'd have his pimple cap on and if he saw us he'd take it off, he wouldn't let me see him in his hat.

It just went from there really. It wasn't an escape for me because we were quite content at home, me and my couple of brothers who still lived there. But George used to make me laugh. As I say, we were all in a group, and then on a Saturday night we used to babysit his brother Ricky – who was twelve years old, believe it or not. His mum and dad were both hard workers and they would go round the pub on a Saturday night. We'd go round to his house, and the brother we were supposed to be babysitting would be out half the bleeding time. But I had to be in at ten o'clock. The pubs used to shut at half past ten then so George would see me home. I *had to be* in on time.

He was one of two kids that were really quite spoilt. He had a lovely family, and they made wonderful in-laws. He's got a cousin who was a policeman, another one who was a priest, all in the same family.

When I was fifteen, just under sixteen, we'd been going out for a year. His mum and dad were going away and they said, "Would you like to come with us?" My mum was a bit funny about it, so she had to go round to see his mum, but I went away with them to Jaywick in Essex.

George was very respectful to my dad. My dad used to say

he was a gentleman. I don't know what he'd have fucking thought of him now! But the first time George ever met my mum, she was having a fight with the woman downstairs. He said, "Is *that* your mum?"

Even when we were married, George would come home from work and my mum would say, "Go down the shop for me, boy."

"No, send one of my brothers," I'd speak up for him.

"Oh, they've been at work all day."

"Well so has he!"

If he didn't want to go he should have been straight and said so. But he wouldn't disrespect her. My mum thought a lot of him, and he loved my mum's cooking. She used to make a lovely curry, and because she'd mixed with a lot of Jewish people she could make gefilte and her own chopped liver. She was a beautiful cook, I miss my mum's cooking.

Anyway, I was at the laundry till I was seventeen, after I fell pregnant with my daughter. I was there nearly a couple of years before I found out I was having Deana.

I was seventeen in May 1958. We got married in June and George was seventeen in July. So at the time of our marriage lines he was sixteen. It seems strange now, a sixteen-year-old getting married, but we didn't have clubs and the kind of life that they live now.

Got married in June, had Deana in October. In those days it was a case of, "He'll have to marry you." But I'll give his dad his due, he asked George, "Do you want to get married?" And George said, "Yeah." I was never asked back then, I wasn't given a choice. My mum took it well really though. And because my dad liked George he was alright, but he was just a miserable man – though a very smart one, never went out without a trilby and a cravat, and a mac or an overcoat.

THE WARS OF ROSIE

My dad did get better as he got older, and he became more amiable with his grandchildren. But when I was first married, I lived with my mum and dad for a little while. He was back at work then, floor laying. He'd come in, wash his hands, go in the bathroom and be in bed by seven o'clock. And then it was, "*Sshh*, turn that telly down, he's in bed." I'd say, "I'm never going to *sshh*," and I never did. When my kids were little I'd have the Hoover on.

But my mum would go, "He's in bed, he's on the warpath." He was a funny man. The only time he was amiable was if he'd had a drink. He was quite chatty then, he became a different person really. (I was eight when my Nanny Dean had died, my dad's mother. I know you shouldn't speak ill of the dead but she was a piss artist.) Pubs didn't interest my mum. If she had a drink she'd have a neat gin, in a tiny little glass like an eyeglass, but she wasn't a drinker. I've seen my mum take my dad's dinner into the pub and aim it at him!

My dad never said to you, "Would you make us a cup of tea?" He'd go, "*Make me a cup of tea!*" You'd get up and you wouldn't dare say no. He couldn't stand laziness, you couldn't be lazy around him. If my brothers were out of work, they had to go and sell something. My mum's money always had to be there, which is right. When I hear people say, "My wossname started work, I don't take nothing off him," they're not giving them responsibility. I took money off my kids – though they certainly had it back in other ways.

My mum lived till she was nearly eighty. But my dad was sixty-three when he died, he was young really. I think my dad was a couple of months younger than my mum. They say opposites attract: my mum was the fighter and my dad would stay in the background. Physically though, he used to be able

31

to have a fight. She said that, when he was young, "I've seen them frogmarch your father along Bethnal Green." He was a bastard then, but as he got older he became more ill.

My mum had some funny sayings. "Never trust anyone with ginger hair!" Or if you brought anyone in: "Don't fetch that one here no more, she's too forward."

"But Mum, she's . . ."

"No, I don't want her in here no more. Never trust anyone with a cast in their eye."

Oh, she was funny! My kids used to laugh at her: "*Oh Nan!*" But a lot of what my mum used to say came true. She had a very good sixth sense.

When I got married, my mother-in-law bought my wedding ring and she said to me, "You can have a thin twenty-two-carat wedding ring or a wide nine-carat ring." I said, "I'll have the wide one."

The day I got married, my mum said, "You'll never have a day's luck with that wedding ring."

That's a horrible thing to say. But it's funny how things turn out, isn't it?

2

LOVE AND MARRIAGE

I was living with my mother-in-law when we first got
married. When George left school he started work in a
wood factory, and then a job came up as a lighterman.[1] But
they used to give lightermen £5 a week and that money
couldn't keep us. So he had to give that job up, on the
understanding with our families that, in a few years, he
could go back.

Of course they never kept their word, so he went to work
in a builder's yard. If that happened today and that was your
kid, you'd say, "We'll manage somehow, don't lose your
job." But neither his parents nor mine said that.

I was still working. I worked till I was eight and a half
months pregnant on the bloody big presses, when he started
work for a little builder's merchant's. Deana was born in
October '58, on the twelfth. (Half of twelve is six –
remember my numbers?) We were living with my mother-in-

---

1 *Lightermen were a fixture of the Port of London for several hundred years –
named for the craft they operated on the river (lighters), they used a combination
of muscle and skill to transport goods from ship to quayside.*

law until Deana was about three months old. Without being disrespectful, and as much as I loved my mother-in-law, they never had a bathroom and I'd been used to that for the past ten years of my life at least.

Then one of my brothers got married and my dad decorated the bedroom, so I moved back with my mum. And then we got a place over at the Isle of Dogs, when Deana was about fourteen or fifteen months old. To give my mother- and father-in-law their dues, they took me out and bought two fireside chairs – we never had a three-piece – and a table and four chairs. I thought it was ever so posh. George's cousin used to do Marley tiles and he tiled the bathroom, kitchen and toilet.

Oh, it was funny on the island, I'd say that was one of the happiest times, and yet I hated it there, *hated* it.

We lived at number sixteen Triton House, with one bedroom. As you walked in, you had the toilet, then you had to walk through a door where you had the coal bunker, the cooker and the bath. You could sit in the bath and watch the telly in the front room.

We'd only been there about a month when there was a knock on the door and a little boy standing there. "Mum said have you got any dog-ends she can roll up?" I *laughed*. I'd heard it all then.

In those days you used to pay your rent fortnightly. I always put mine away, but the neighbours would borrow your rent. They'd always give it back to you, they were lovely people, the salt of the earth. But because I had a bit of fitted Cyril Lord carpet I used to pay ten bob a month for, they thought I was posh.

We had some laughs over there with some of the characters. But I didn't like it, I felt cut off. Because of the bridges, only the 56 and 277 buses used to go there. It was like the stagecoach coming along every bloody couple of days. But you couldn't wish for lovelier people. They were poor, but they all helped one another.

We weren't even there for two years, but there wasn't much of a social scene really. You didn't go out in pubs – well, we certainly didn't. I think I was twenty-one before I had my first drink in a pub. (My granddaughters laugh at me now: "*How old were you?*") If I went down the pub to my dad, I'd open the door and call him out, I'd never walk inside.

I used to say to George when we first got married, "Why don't you go out and have a drink?" "I don't know what your brothers see in drink," he'd say. He knows now.

My brother Colin, who I buried the other week, was a compere years ago. He was handsome when he was young, a big fellah, all the girls used to be after him. He knocked Michael Barrymore out along the Old Kent Road because they used to compete in different pubs. Barrymore was just up and coming then, and my Colin said he was really flash. But my brother could give a song and if he was singing in a pub we'd go down there.

We were in our early twenties then, but George wasn't a drinker. I don't know when he really got the taste for it. Of course then we never had the money for him to go out.

But it wasn't a bad time. You just plod along, don't you? I would say they were the most contented years, to be honest. I wasn't at work then, but I got a little job cutting cottons off for my sister who was in dressmaking at Aldgate.

George wasn't earning good money, but it wasn't bad money, it kept us. To me, contentment was getting your wages on a Friday, putting your bill money away and knowing you were alright for another week. Paying your way and owing nothing. I was quite a contented person, I was never one that suffered with my nerves. I'd go to work, come home, do what I had to do, sit and watch the telly. I didn't want the high life, I was satisfied to go out once or twice a month to the local. I didn't want the stars.

I hate debt, even now. If you work for something, you treasure it more than when it's easy come, easy go. If I went to bingo – not that I've been very lucky with bingo – and won a couple of bob, I'd squander it, I didn't think twice.

George wasn't a flash bloke. Every photo I have of that time, he's always in the background. He was never one to be up the front, he was unassuming really. George didn't like confrontation. Physically, he could knock you spark out – though I've never really seen him fight. When the kids were little they'd argue with the other kids, but if anyone had to go sort it out it was me. Mentally, if you speak to anyone they'll all say, "Georgie was a nice fellah but he didn't want to be disliked." Sooner than argue with someone, he'd agree with them. But you've got to have an opinion, haven't you?

I don't think you'd meet anyone that would say a bad word about him. Everyone liked him. But I'm sorry, you can't be nice all the time, can you? If someone is nice to me all the time then there's something the matter with them. They get a bit too sweet to be wholesome.

One time he did show he'd got a mind of his own. The only interest I ever showed in politics was going to vote once, when I was twenty-one. (We weren't allowed to vote before then.) I voted Labour because my mum and dad voted Labour. When I came out, George said he'd voted Conservative. I went, "Oh, don't dare let my mum and dad hear you!"

"Why?"

"My dad will go mental! He says the Conservatives are

only for people with shops. What have you got to conserve?" I thought Conservatives were just for people who had their own property.

Like I say, you've got to have your own opinion, but it was weird how it came out of George just that once. He was clever. He could have worked in an office, he could have done anything. But no.

George was a good dad in the early years, I can't take that away from him. When we moved to Belton Way, off of Bow Common Lane, in 1962, Deana was three or four.

In '63 I was having another baby. In those days you didn't have scans and things like that. I never did a day's work when I was having him, not one day, but he was a breach birth. They wouldn't let it happen today, they'd give you a caesarean, but I had hypnosis to try and turn him. He came bottom first, so they knew it was a boy before I'd even had him.

He was born with spina bifida. Five minutes after, they rushed him away. The chief gynaecologist at Mile End Hospital – whose daughter was Heather Sears, who played the deaf and blind girl in that film, *The Story of Esther Costello* – came and said, "We're taking the baby to Great Ormond Street, but before we do we'll christen him." So we christened him Mark.

He laid in the hospital. I used to go, but I didn't go every day. They told me that with spina bifida the water goes to the head, so the head gets bigger and bigger. He grew like a normal baby, but I used to feed him with his little body on the cot while I held his head in my arms. When he died they drew all the water off of him.

You couldn't buy him anything, obviously. But there was a little girl there who'd been fostered out, she'd got frostbite and lost both her feet. Oh, she was a pretty little thing with her blonde hair. I got very attached to Sally, I'd love to know how she is now. Mark would have been forty-five, she's got to be forty-eight or forty-nine. She used to wait for me, I'd take sweets up for her.

Me and George's aunt bought her a doll when they first started selling toys at Boot's the Chemist. When I took it in there the priest came in, he wanted to anoint the baby. I said yeah, he could do it. She went to him, "Men don't wear dresses!" The priest laughed. I said, "I've got something for you in this bag. It's yours."

"Mine? To keep?" She had false feet and she used to toddle along in her little boots.

But once the baby died I couldn't go back there. It was sad, because Deana knew at that age, but how do you explain to a kid? She was looking forward to a baby coming home, but he was in the hospital all the time. I don't think I ever took her to see him.

I always followed what my mum said in terms of traditions. When you had a baby, you came out of hospital and went to church to thank God that you'd got over it. You didn't have to be religious, it was just a thing that you always did.

But of course there was nothing they could do for the baby. He only lived three months, almost to the day. He was born on the sixth of October and died on the seventh of January. You see what I'm saying about those numbers?

I wasn't on the phone then, and my friend who lived in the flats facing us gave them her phone number. Her husband come over early on the Sunday morning to tell me he'd died.

I went to bingo that week, I suppose because I'd been told he wasn't going to live. You were prepared for it, which is different to a sudden death. We didn't have a pot to piss in, and I won twelve pounds ten – exactly how much the undertaker wanted. Mark was buried in Bow Church.

Even then George couldn't face it. He only went up to the hospital a couple of times. I suppose men are different to women like that. I really don't know. But I had Deana to think of. You have to pick yourself up and get on with it, don't you?

When I lost that baby I needed something to occupy my mind. His aunt, who lived along the landing, said, "They're looking for someone to wash up at the Globe in Moorgate." It's still there now, a great big pub. Mr McGinty, the governor, asked if I'd like a waitress's job. "Oh no, I can't do that," I said, "I'll be alright washing up."

My mother-in-law and all her family were waitresses, but I thought it wasn't for me at that time. Anyway, I got the job, four pounds a week, Monday to Friday, eleven till half past two. The four waitresses were really good to me. I used to run up and down the stairs to get drinks for their customers, and on a Friday one used to buy me forty fags while another gave me five shillings. It all made my money up. (There were cheap fares then too, a lot cheaper than what they bloody well are now!)

I just used to do the washing up and keep the little kitchen clean. Then I came in one morning and he said, "Rose, would you like to do an extra hour? We've got live-in bar staff, we need someone to change the beds." Well it was another extra pound, it'd pay another bill. That's how I had to think in those days.

I said I'd do it on a trial, but oh, the stink of sweat and food. I only did it to help them out until they got someone. Then one day a waitress was out and he asked if I'd like to do that. I didn't think I could, but I ended up earning thirty bob in tips. I couldn't believe it. I never looked back from that day, I went waitressing whenever I could.

And then Ricky came in '65, on his father's birthday, seventeenth of July. (His daughter's got the same birthday now – so that's granddad, son and granddaughter.) Deana was seven in the October. When he was little it was always, "I'll go and get my big sister!" He was a lovely little boy though. He didn't like you telling him off, but I never had to smack him really.

I smacked *her*, she was a cheeky little cow when she was getting older. My mother- and father-in-law were too bleeding soft on her at times. As a little girl she put on weight, so I took her to a dietician in London. The doctor advised us to stick to a diet but she'd go over to my mother-in-law's and have big cream cakes, undoing what I'd done. If she ate one, she'd probably have two or three. She was a good girl, don't get me wrong, but she was a real one for her food.

George was lorry driving then for Robinson's from their Thomas Street depot in Bow, from when Ricky was three months old. We were just about getting by when a pub job came up in the Cottons. (They've just pulled that pub down actually. It wasn't that old.). His aunt who lived along there said, "They're looking for a cleaner, but you've got to do seven mornings a week." That suited me, I could take the baby with me.

Deana went to the school round the corner from the pub, so I used to take the two of them with me on a weekday, and at nine o'clock the governor would let me leave the baby there. I'd run her round the corner and come back. My Rick would be sitting at the table with a few little toys, he was an angel as a kid. (Deana was a cow! If she had a pair of scissors she used to cut the corners off everything; she never had a doll with hair on its head.) I worked there till Rick started nursery school five years later. If they had an artiste on Saturday night, they'd go in one bar and let me clean up, to save me going in on Sunday morning. I used to get an extra six pounds a week, which was good money. You could get a lovely bit of beef for twelve and six.

GEORGE DAVIS

We were just an ordinary sort of couple going about our lives, you know. We went out weekends and sometimes we'd have a couple of drinks, and that was it. We enjoyed one another's company. I mean, we had rows as with any couple. But from when we originally got married and had nothing, we both worked and gradually got together a nice little home. We were quite content with our two children.

My Rick was about two when my dad died, so I'd have been about twenty-four, quite young really. My dad was young too, only about sixty-three. He died in St Joseph's Hospice. I can remember going in the ambulance with him, he said, "My feet are cold, girl." So I put a pair of socks on him and got him to the hospice.

Once you're in there you can have what you want, so I brought him a little bottle of brandy. He said, "Don't let them see it!" I said, "Oh, they won't say anything!" Of course I didn't tell him the full extent of why he was in there. He thought he had an ulcer, he didn't know he had cancer of the stomach. In those days doctors weren't so forward. They told my mum, but my mum said, "Don't dare tell him that!" They'd only given him six months to live, but he'd lived for nearly two years. It was sheer willpower really.

I went in the hospice the day after he was admitted, with my mum. "The television people came in here yesterday," he said, "they wanted to interview me but I didn't want to be interviewed." "Oh," I thought, "his mind's wandering." Six months later, I was sitting watching the telly and they were there, in the hospice. It was really weird.

He was only in there a few days and he died. My dad's was only the third funeral I'd ever been to – after my nan's, and the baby I lost between Deana and Rick.

When Rick went to school, my sister was working at Plantation House in Mincing Lane. She used to do eleven till three and she said to me they were looking for a waitress. I tried it, and I soon found out which customers you could have a joke with and who you couldn't.

Matthew Harding use to come in there when he very first went into the City, the multimillionaire Chelsea supporter who got killed in a helicopter. He used to leave me two bob, which was a bloody good tip then. He was a lovely fellah, we used to have some laughs with him. He finished up married with kids, then he had an affair with a waitress and she had a little girl.

Then I started doing the banquets, and I got greedy. George hated me working nights, but I was only 'greedy' in the sense of, "That'll pay this bill. We need this and that'll pay for that . . ."

I don't think he was worried about my safety, though he used to take me out to work. I used to laugh because I sat with girls who were obviously quite comfortably off, whose husbands had good jobs. They used to say, "I don't have to work, you know. This is *my* money." I'd say, "Oh, my husband gets me ready for work." It was their pin money, whereas I had to live on it. I don't know if George appreciated that. Looking back now, I do blame a lot of what happened later on myself. I never gave him any responsibility.

I was probably too strong for George. He couldn't say to me, "You're not going," if there was a beano at work the next week. It was a red rag to a bull. I'm true to my sign, I'm a Taurus. Don't tell me I can't do something, because then I *will*. So he gave up in the end.

Really, it was only through me that he got to know Mickey Ishmail. I first met Jeannie Ishmail when we moved to Belton Way. She lived in a mobile home facing us, which you could see as you stood on my balcony. I used to hang a bit of washing out, and I'd see Jeannie with her three little girls, pretty little girls, all dressed the same.

One night there was a knock on the door and she was standing there. I didn't know her name then. She said, "You've got a little boy, ain't you?" I said yeah. She was selling some trousers. I didn't ask questions, just said, "Oh yeah, I'll have a couple of pairs." I put them away, they were too big for him.

I saw her down the shop, just made general chit-chat and whatever. Then, when I was working in the pub, we'd gone out for a drink one night with George's cousin and her husband and in walked Jeannie, her husband and some other company.

At the end of the evening she came over. "My husband said would you like to come to a club with us?" We didn't have a lot of money, but I always carried my rent with me just in case. I'm going back many years ago, but for four quid you could go and have a good drink and a meal.

I was thinking of a working man's club, which I'd been to before, but it was the Starlight Rooms at Tottenham. Of course there were women in evening dress, and I had my little twenty-five-bob blouse and skirt on. Marty Wilde was up there, trying to make a comeback, Joe Brown too.[2]

George kicked me under the table. "Have you got the rent?" Because the bill had come round. "Have you got five?"

"What, five minutes?"

But I passed him a fiver under the table so he could put his bit on – he was never mugged-off in that respect. They knew we never had anything, but I wouldn't have ponced, and nor would he. It was the first nightclub I'd ever been to, and it was the start of a friendship.

(I got very, very close to Jeannie, but years later she stabbed me in the back. I can't say why, but believe me, it hurt. She has never faced me about it. Perhaps she will after this book comes out.)

Mickey Ishmail had a reputation, and I know that better than anyone. Jeannie was a good, clean mum, but those kids had a terrible upbringing. He'd come home and knock her about, and they would be laying in bed listening to it. They've got to have been disturbed by it in their own way, because it was a continual thing. Those girls are all bundles of nerves. It's sad, because they were three lovely girls of about fourteen, twelve and eleven at the time, but you can't tell me it hasn't affected them. Can you imagine what they were laying in bed thinking? It's got to do something to you, like those people who have flashbacks of bad accidents. Men like that never know what they've done to their kids mentally, not till they grow up.

---

2 *Marty Wilde and Joe Brown were the original breed of 1950s Brit-rock 'n' roll stars, managed by Tin Pan Alley impresario Larry Parnes. Parnes' stable were mostly watered-down versions of the American originals, but Brown's more authentic sound won him club audiences for decades.*

Mine never had that, I would *not* have allowed it. No way would I have ever let my kids go through that, and I can't understand women who do. You see it every day on the telly, you think, "What are you, a fucking doormat?"

I'd see Jeannie with a black eye the next day, bashed up, wearing dark glasses. Or she'd wake me up at two o'clock in the morning with the kids. She'd walk out, I'd put them all up, and then the next night she'd be down the pub with him.

I used to say to her, "Whatever do you put up with it for?" But some women do, don't they? I wouldn't have stood one black eye, let alone twenty. "I don't want to be on my own," she said. I'd sooner be on my own. It wasn't like he was bringing her home a grand every week and she had to stay there for it. She must have been a bit touched.

It's easy for me to say that, I know, because I've never been frightened of anyone. But some women are. George was never abusive, he wouldn't have dared. He might have hit me once and got away with it. He wouldn't have done it twice.

Mind you, we used to laugh. I used to say to her, "I tell you what I'd do: I'd boil a kettle, wait for him to come home pissed, and I'd pour it right between his legs!"

And I would have. I don't think anyone's got the right to tell someone else what to do, to dictate to them what they can wear. *No.*

RICK DAVIS

Mickey Ishmail was a horrible man, a horrible flash bastard. I remember we were up there once, the girls were literally pissing themselves in fear of him. He beat Jeannie up, he was right horrible. My dad would never have laid a hand on me.

But then you've got to look at the other side of it. On one particular day, the middle daughter was back after running away from home for a fortnight or whatever. Jeannie knocked at the door and said, "I've had to come over here, I've left Jackie with him, he's going to give her a good hiding."

I'll never forget that. I went, "You've left him with Jackie? I'm sorry Jeannie, but he'd have to come through me first to get to her." I was speaking as a mother. She was scared of him, and I know different people react in different ways. I couldn't imagine Rick's father saying to me, "Get out of the house, I'm going to sort him out!" He'd have to sort me out first.

Yet if you met Mickey he was good company, he made you laugh. He was a charmer. But the other side of him . . .

He had his good side, and I never saw that dark side of him. I've got to speak as I find. He was liked and he was hated. He liked the women. I don't know how many girlfriends he had but she knew about them, and she had him back. I mean *come on*, show a bit of self-respect. I think he's got about five kids, including the three daughters that I know.

I hate any man who's a bully, I don't care who he is. But I'd take ten of Mickey over one of Jeannie. I'd trust him with my life if he was still here today. I didn't like what he did to her, but then she stood for it. But personally I couldn't fault Mickey.

Jeannie told me in conversation that her husband worked on the oil rigs. I soon put two and two together – he was in prison for receiving stolen goods, that sort of thing, though he was obviously on home leave by the time we met him. It was none of my business. All that crowd were good company, they didn't interfere with my life.

My mum had been a wheeler and dealer, that's how she brought us up, though she wasn't a thief. She got arrested for twelve bottles of gin she'd bought off someone to make a profit when she sold them on. In those days you had to take your rent book up the police station. "Oh my God, I'm not going up no police station!" said my dad. He gave me the rent book and I took it up Bow Road nick. I must have been fourteen or fifteen.

It was twelve bottles of water that she'd been sold. You can imagine what her language was like when she came out! Still, they couldn't nick her for bottles of water.

In those days, if anyone knocked at the door with anything you didn't question it, it was an accepted thing in the East End. "Come off the back of a lorry," was all you'd hear. Today you might question it, today you might *know*.

Out of curiosity though, I said to Jeannie, "What's it like?" I'd never had any dealings with the police and I'd never seen the inside of a prison. She said, "I'm going in to see a friend of Mickey's," it was Johnny Shea, who I think at that time had been shot in the hand and had something to do with the Krays, "you can come with me if you want to." So the first time I ever went to Brixton Prison was with Jeannie.

He was in top security, and they were fetching the Kray brothers through, that shows how long ago it was.[3] They were running the Krays up the stairs. I said, "Aren't they funny, the police in here?" Jeannie said, "They're not *police*!" That's how naïve I was, I thought the screws were coppers.

I also went once to see Mickey in Chelmsford, I think he was in for receiving. Of course she knew the ropes, because

---

3 *Ronnie and Reggie Kray were remanded to HMP Brixton on three charges of murder in May 1968, remaining there until they received life sentences on two of the counts in February 1969.*

of Mickey being in and out of prison. I didn't, but I learned soon enough. It really opened my eyes. I got shrewder, I got very well educated. Little did I know that, a few years later, I'd be going backwards and forwards myself. They're not nice places, prisons, especially not for taking kids.

3

STAND BY
YOUR MAN

When George started going out drinking on Sunday lunchtimes, I was very content just to go to work, come home and see to my family. He liked a drink, but then he started drinking heavier. He liked Mickey Ishmail's company, and Mickey liked his. Mickey was a likeable character, he made you laugh, he could tell a story. And then he went home and bashed Jeannie up. You couldn't put the two people together.

George was a working man up to 1972, and then he lost his licence for two years over drink-driving in his old Comma van. In those days it was a disgrace to lose your licence, and obviously he lost his job with it. From then on it was nothing much, apart from a bit of mini-cabbing. His working life stopped there. Full stop.

I thought he'd go out and get a job, though not driving obviously. "I ain't working for that poxy money," he'd say.

On a Friday, there was a thing I always did from the day we got married. I had a tin where I'd put the rent away, the insurance, everything that had to be paid. That was my comfort zone.

He'd borrow out of the tin. I knew how much he borrowed. But when Friday came and he'd give me his wages, he'd put back what was in the tin and go, "Look, I've worked all the week for that." Perhaps it would be £1 or twenty-five bob. I'd say, "Yeah, but that's yours. I ain't got twenty-five bob to spend on *me*. What I've got in my purse is keeping the home." But he could never see it.

I quickly got the message that he wasn't going out to work again. He'd borrow a car and do a bit of cabbing. He fiddled and diddled, but I never asked questions. I was just getting on with my life. Going to work, coming home, doing what you have to do. I must have been content because I wouldn't have put up with it otherwise, would I?

He was done once for receiving, three or four cameras if I remember rightly. It was the same old story, I didn't ask questions. "Someone asked me to mind them," he said, and I just left it at that. I didn't think, "Oh, they're stolen!" I was very naïve. But when you've not been brought up with that way of life, you don't know any different, do you?

GEORGE

As I said, we just had a normal life. There were local pubs we'd go in and parties with local people. And then I lost my driving licence and it was different. I was a lorry driver, so once I lost my driving licence let's just say I strayed.

The first time I got nicked as an adult, I got a three-month suspended sentence for receiving some electrical goods which had been taken in a burglary.

But I was never someone who stood out in a crowd. I'd go unnoticed. People would know me but they wouldn't know my name. Which was very good, actually. There was always a possibility that they would have known Rose rather than me.

THE WARS OF ROSIE

In the East End you knew all the villains by association. I grew up with Mickey Calvey, who the police shot when he was doing a supermarket over the other side of the water.[1] Mickey was the nicest, smartest fellah, but you wouldn't like to cross him. We all grew up as kids and if I'd have been a boy and I'd have got in trouble, they would have said it was down to association with people like him. That's the way of the world.

I knew Mickey's wife, Linda, well before she married him. She's away now. Linda was quite a nice girl actually, from what I knew of her. But they led a very strange life, him and her. She was a lovely looking girl, but she was one of them who goes [simpering], "*Oh 'ello. You alright?*" You would never, ever in a million years think her capable of doing away with anybody.[2] But it's always the quiet ones, isn't it?

She left two kids and she's got grandchildren, it's so sad. What a waste of life. Silly girl, but there you are.

Anyway, that was really the start of mine and George's problems. Maybe, with Mickey Ishmail wheeling and dealing, he thought, "Oh well, that's easy money!" I don't know. I never discussed that sort of thing with him.

---

1 *Calvey was shot dead during a police ambush in 1978. The policeman who fired the fatal shots into his back stood trial, facing a cry of "Murderer!" from Calvey's widow Linda. The officer was acquitted and commended for bravery.*

2 *Linda Calvey, infamous as 'the Black Widow', had already served time on conspiracy charges before being sentenced to life for the murder of her lover, armed robber Ronnie Cook, in 1990. According to Daniel Reece, the convicted rapist she hired for the hit, she shot Cook point-blank through the head when he couldn't go through with it. Such betrayal didn't stop her making Reece her second husband, marrying him in prison in 2002. In August 2008, sixty-year-old Linda was paroled after seventeen years of her sentence.*

Another man would have gone and found any kind of work. He'd done a variety of jobs, even humping coal, which was bloody hard work. Instead, him and Mickey opened an unlicensed drinking club down Devons Road. It was in a normal house; Peter Chappell had the downstairs as a second-hand shop and they had the upstairs. They'd open Friday, Saturday and Sunday and every drink was ten bob. They'd go and buy it in the off licence and they earned a living that way. This was when the pubs used to shut at half past ten, which was when people would come knocking. But the house belonged to a church and then they found out. They weren't very pleased.

PETER CHAPPELL

I think I first came across George round about 1972. I was in the haulage business and independent of all the crooks and the villains. I made my own good living. So I could stand toe-to-toe in that respect in their company, in pubs and places like that. I was on a par with them, I was my own man. We used to play cards in Jimmy Murphy's pub of a Saturday morning, the Dover Castle in Sutton Street. George didn't play cards but Mickey Ishmail did. The rest of the pub would be running as a normal public house but we had a little card school in the corner. They were mates of Jimmy's and I was a mate of Jimmy's. When I'd go in there of a weekend with the wife, we'd all be in the same sort of company. It's well known that these chaps do have a certain appeal, even though they're crooks or whatever, they do have a certain charisma.

I don't think Ishmail knew Davis very much longer than I did, maybe two or three years. George was a working boy, HGV driver. He use to work off the island for a tipper firm,

*I think. Somehow or other he got webbed up with Ishmail,
but he was a straight-up working man until he met him. I
don't think he had a conviction or anything. His mother and
father were respectable working-class people. Never in a bit
of trouble in their lives, brought their children up properly.
And it just all went fucking wrong with that bastard.*

*Mickey Ishmail hated the police. It was quite a healthy
hatred because I've never had much time for them, although
I've come across the odd one that I'd be happy to have a
drink with. But on the whole, I didn't like him very much.
Very flash bloke, lots of charisma, but he would dominate
you if he got the opportunity. As with many people like that,
he had that sort of air about him. It's my opinion that he
dominated George to quite a degree, and anyone else that
got really close to him. He was the guv'nor, no two ways
about it. But to anyone that could stand their own ground,
he showed a healthy respect. He could be quite sinister. He
had that look about him, a tall, slim Yiddish lad with
Yiddish mannerisms.*

GEORGE

*Mickey wasn't Jewish! He used to make out he was a Jew.
His old man came out of Canning Town. I think he just used
to say it to get good food.*

PETER

*You never saw Mickey without a glass in his hand and a pair
of tinted shades. People wanted to know him, wanted to be
in his company. All sorts of people, small businessmen,
publicans. But he used that, he'd have an edge on them. Not
Jimmy Murphy – he'd be one of the people that Mickey
would have a healthy respect for. But if there was a*

weakness in you, he'd try and exploit it. Not a very nice bloke. I always kept Mickey at arm's length.

I can remember one time, not long before they picked him up for the London Electricity Board robbery at Ilford, he'd just got off a charge from the Old Bailey – something to do with stealing from some railway arches. George had just got off too, and they'd had a falling out. I'd heard Mickey had banged him in the face quite violently. I can remember saying to George, "Why don't you come and work with me? You're a lorry driver – we'll go halves, everything I get I'll split down the middle with you. Come and get away from all this." No.

GEORGE

Before April '74, I'd already been nicked for conspiracy to steal goods from a railway yard in Leytonstone. Me, Mickey Ishmail and some others were acquitted on the twenty-ninth of March. But I had another charge arising out of that, driving while disqualified. I went back to the Old Bailey and they offered no evidence against me, so it was thrown out. This was on the twenty-third of April.

The LEB robbery in Ilford had occurred on the fourth of April. It was big news. Everyone saw it because of the chase. That week, I was signing on and I went to do a bit of mini-cabbing, because I never had any money. I was using my brother's car. I only did it that week, for four days. My brother wanted me to pay him for the car and I wouldn't, so that was the end of that.

So come the twenty-third of April, I go up to the Bailey. Detective Sergeant Peter West, who'd been involved in the case, said, "I'm going to come round your house tomorrow," bringing back the stuff which they'd taken in the original search. I was home that afternoon and two

*police officers arrived. I said, "Did Peter West send you?"
They went, "Well, indirectly. We've come about a robbery in
Ilford." That's when they first arrested me.*

*They took me to Ilford police station. I gave them my
alibi and they let me go home. I think we may well have
gone into the cab office, because Terry Calvey, Mickey
Calvey's brother, had the office book and they may have
wanted to see whether my name was there.*

*So that was that. Cleared. End of. Never thought any more
of it. Then, early in the morning on the fourth of May, they
came in with guns and pulled us in again to Ilford. There was
me, Mickey, Tommy Hole, Roy Daniels and my brother,
Ricky. Once again they asked for our alibis. They let us go
about midday. I thought, "That's it, it's finally over."*

*Nearly a fortnight later, on the seventeenth of May, they
came round, arrested me and Mick again and took us into
Walthamstow police station for robbery of the
Walthamstow Guardian. They put me and Mick on
identification parade. I didn't get picked out, but Mick did.
George England had already been picked out. And then they
said we're going to hold you overnight for ID on the Ilford
robbery. The next day they did the ID and I got picked out
three times. I was charged with the robbery at Ilford.*

*Apparently they were going all over London, pulling
people in. We applied for bail but got blanked, because of the
seriousness of the offence. I always remember that the
following Sunday was baking hot. One of the sergeants came
out and said, "Come on, I'll get you a bit of air." He took me
into this big room and opened the window to get some fresh
air. So I said, "'Ere, you know I ain't done this?" "Yeah," he
said, "we know that, but it'll all come out in the wash."*

We got remanded in custody. The funny part was that

*Tommy Hole came up and visited me and Mick in there. The
next thing you know, they've nicked him for the same thing. I
don't know how many times Tom got picked out. But the only
one in trouble was me, because I had the most IDs against me.
Five policemen ID'd me out of thirty-nine witnesses.*

*We were all nicked for armed robbery and two attempted
murders of policemen. One, PC Grove, was shot in the leg.
The other one got knocked up in the air, I think he broke
his leg or something when they were escaping in the car.
They dropped that one, said it was a pure accident. Then,
with PC Grove, they took it down to wounding with intent
to resist arrest.*

George got arrested on the seventeenth of May 1974, a
Friday – I know that because my birthday was on the
following Sunday. The robbery was on the fourth of April,
but by now we were in May.

I didn't even know the LEB raid had happened. The police
came early that morning and they turned the place over.
Bang! Bang! Bang! They don't knock lightly. He got up and
answered the door. Even then the penny didn't drop. "Who's
that this time of the morning?" But then I heard all the
voices and I got up. They just went all over the house. I
didn't even ask what they were searching for.

As I was getting ready to come downstairs, I could hear,
"We've got a search warrant . . ." I think I went onto
autopilot. And that was the day my life changed, really.

I thought, "What's all this about?" But they don't tell you
anything. They were pulling everything out and they didn't
put anything back. Instead of it registering that they'd
arrested him, I'm thinking, "I've got to clear all this up!" I
think I was in shock.

They took George that morning and that was it. There was no bail, nothing. Peter Chappell came round to me, so he must have heard through the grapevine that Mickey and all of them had been arrested.

Afterwards, Peter went to the police to say he'd seen George on the morning of the robbery. Jeannie Ishmail and me went to Ilford police station with him. On the way there was a couple in a car who had a fight with us at the lights. What a turnout that was. This bloke had cut Peter up badly, he could have caused a bad accident. Peter got out and said, "You *stupid* . . ." We all got out of the car and we were all fighting. We were at a set of traffic lights; Jeannie jumped out because she was nearer the door; the woman jumped out; the woman's gone for Jeannie and Jeannie's pulled her hair, and as she did it turned out to be a wig! And then her kid got out and he was kicking me.

When we got to the police station they let us go into the cell. George looked like death warmed up. He was yellow. He'd had a real shock to the system. He was due to appear in court on the following Monday and he was holding it together, but I should imagine he was bloody scared. He was talking to you but he wasn't with you. "You've got to get me out of here . . ." I looked at Peter, and said, "We're not going to let you rot. We'll do all we can." But at that stage I didn't realise Pete would go to the lengths he did. Or my brothers.

Peter got the full details on the charges. I think the police knew I wasn't used to dealing with this sort of thing. Even having all those brothers, they never brought that sort of trouble home to my mum. They weren't angels, and I can remember my brother getting arrested for an affray with two other boys. But my brothers couldn't come home and tell my dad. My mum knew, but he'd have gone absolutely spare. And George, when he was fourteen or fifteen, did the same thing with some boys down Crisp Street. His father went mad. He went to court and was put on probation. That was his first brush with the police, but it was just part of growing up. It wasn't for thieving or anything like that.

Of course, you try to protect your kids. Deana had just started work then, and it wasn't reported in the press yet. "Where's Daddy?" "Oh, he won't be long."

When they had the committal for trial at Waltham Forest, it was a slog getting there every day. I couldn't go to work; I had to go over the café to order their dinners. I don't know if he realised the extent of what went on. I don't think a man would do for a woman what a woman would do for a man. I honestly don't. I could never see him doing it for me.

If you were to see the photos that a passer-by was supposed to have taken,[3] I've always said that the police genuinely thought they had the right people. I really do believe that. Because if you looked at those photos, you couldn't see the faces but the way they were standing would make you say, "Yeah, that's George." I would definitely say it myself.

Tommy Hole wasn't very tall. The fellah that had the gun wasn't very tall. But the one they thought was George had a flying helmet on which wouldn't even go on George's head.

And then, the more and more we delved into it, the more it seemed that the police had verballed them.[4] Why would you

---

3 *The photos were taken by Bob Appleton, an off-duty police constable. As with his friend, the wounded PC Brian Grove, he apparently just happened to be in the vicinity at the time.*

4 *'Verballing' is the traditional police custom of attributing off-the-record remarks (i.e. not part of an official statement) to suspects, without any independent corroborating evidence.*

verbal someone if they were guilty? Why would they supposedly say this and say that? You're not really going to say, "Yeah, I did it, but I'm not going to plead guilty," are you?

GEORGE

I always laugh when the guy is supposed to go, "Yeah, I done it, but you've got to get me though, copper," and all that. Like he's said it to a right plum of a policeman who he probably wouldn't even talk to, let alone confess to. The next thing they say is, "This man is a professional criminal," but he gets in the motor and goes, "Yeah, I done it but you'll have to prove it, guv."

I remember someone telling me he was up on a roof, burgling a warehouse, and the policeman reckoned he heard him shout out, "Watch out, Bill, it's Johnny Law!"

We got nicked by the Essex police when Charlie Lowe grassed us,⁵ and their verbals were funny. It was all old-fashioned, they hadn't caught up with the Met. The Met got really good at it, especially the squads. But when the Essex police did it, it was like something copied out of an old book somewhere, or The Blue Lamp.

There were so many of them on the Robbery Squad who were verballing us during the LEB case. It was crap verbal, but they seemed to like it: "Can I have a word with Mick?" "Can I have a word with George?" I laughed when Mick

---

5 *Charlie Lowe, an East End villain known socially to both Mickey Ishmail and George Davis, became a police 'supergrass' in the mid-1970s. In the wake of notorious turncoats Bertie Smalls and Maurice O'Mahoney, a.k.a. 'King Squealer', he was increasingly willing to inform on friends and associates in return for greatly reduced sentences on his own offences (or, it has been suggested, cash rewards).*

got verballed by a guy called Read. He was taking Mick to the nick on his own – that's how bad we were – when Mick supposedly said in the car: "You're a Geordie, ain't you Mr Read?" Now I've never heard him call anyone Mr anything.

"Yeah, that's right, Mick."

"I always think you can trust Geordies."

"Well, Mickey, I think you've got to take people as you find them."

So Mick's got the verbal. "Who is this fucking Read?" We're in a little van the police used to take us to the court. All of a sudden Mick half-recognises him, he's sitting right opposite. Me and Mick are cuffed.

"Are you this Read?"

"Yeah . . ."

"I like Geordies, you cunt? I fucking hate them, and tell whoever fucking did this I'm going to hit them right in the fucking jaw, you Geordie cunt!"

These were 'the untouchables'. There was another occasion when Mick got a tape recorder in. This was unbeknownst to our solicitors or QCs. The police used to crack on about people we knew, so if they talked too loosely we might be able to expose them if anyone got fitted up. This tape was made going backwards and forwards to the nick because the police had to take us for committal at Waltham Forest. They never said anything on the tape, so we got it back out. But they must have had half a smell, as they had the Special Patrol Group minding us.

This cozzer named Simons has come in, he's got the SPG with him. "Right, he said, "we're just going to give you a rub down."

Mick went, "No you ain't."

"What?"

"You fucking ain't. We get rubbed down when we come out the nick and we get rubbed down when we go back in. You ain't fucking rubbing us down."

"You'll see . . ."

Simons has run out. The SPG have shit themselves. Back he comes with another cozzer. "Right, you're going to get rubbed down, or what happens is one or two of you might get hurt."

Mick stepped forward. "I tell you what, there's an empty cell over there – we'll go over there and you can rub me down, we'll see who gets fucking hurt then."

"Hold up, Mick, hold up. We don't want none of that. No, no, no . . ."

He went back out. They shit their fucking selves.

At the committal they had us cuffed up, so it was really awkward for us to write anything down that we disagreed with. This cozzer O'Brien was sitting over on the other side of the room. Mick was making signs and going to him, "You cunt! I'm going to fucking hurt you!" And yet these were the untouchables.

We knew O'Brien from drinking in a pub in east London during the 1970 World Cup. There was a cozzer called Maybury who knew us too. Anyhow, there had been a little bit of an altercation, this geezer pulled half a stroke. We finished having a drink. They all came after us. As they went outside, Mick went bop, *he pinned the geezer, who was about six foot three, bang on the chin, knocked him spark out. Well, the two cozzers ran. I got him on my back, the geezer, we had to run him away, he was spewing all over the fucking place. O'Brien told us this afterwards, he said, "We didn't know what to do. Maybury said, 'They're burying him, he's dead!'"*

That was Mick, he was fucking fearless.

I think they all thought they'd been framed. Every one of them. As time went on and they were all being verballed, that is when I think we started saying they'd been fitted up. None of them were there. None of them had done that robbery. But by then the police had gone too far, because they'd verballed them. How were they going to get out of that? How were they going to explain the verbal? So they had to see it through. They couldn't hold their hands up to it, they'd have mugged themselves off. I used to call them the Lying Squad and the Rubbery Squad.

Peter didn't think George was innocent; he *knew* he was innocent. That is the difference. I believed he was innocent, but I had no proof of it. So he knew more than me really, and I believed him.

PETER

I had the new haulage business and my wife, Shirley, would be in the little second-hand shop we had at the end of Devons Road, near to Bow Road. I had a contract to deliver urgent hospital equipment throughout the country for a firm in Clydebank, Scotland. I'd go up there three days a week. I was getting £1200 a month just on that. Good money for one man and his little 35 cwt truck. I had that for about four years. But in those days I spent my money as quickly as I got it.

I often saw George because he worked at a cab office which was across the road and about fifty yards along from our shop. It was probably round about ten o'clock on this particular morning, I can't remember whether it was a Monday or Friday morning. I was going to have breakfast and I saw him going to his car as he was coming out of the cab office and I asked him if he wanted to come with me. He said, "No, I've got a job to do." I think he had to deliver fish up to the City or somewhere.

I was very angry, because I knew straight away that I'd seen him. It was out of the box for him, being connected with an armed robbery. It had been in the papers, in the Stratford Express *or the* East London Advertiser, *and there were pictures of people being held up in the road. It was like the Wild West, it was a dramatic robbery.*

PC Grove was injured in the leg – it was in the press that he'd been shot. As soon as it went off the police were on them, chasing them up Gants Hill and holding up the traffic. It just didn't gel with my image of George. Then it came to me later on that day that I'd seen him. I immediately took the girls, Jeannie Ishmail and Rose, to the police station out Essex way.

And then very quickly he was charged. It might have been on the Friday, as on the Saturday night I took Rosie straight to Scotland Yard. This is how naïve we were, no fucking about, straight in the front on a Saturday evening. I remember they admitted us into the place and it was very dark, the only lights were coming from the street. Me and Rose were in this big lobby, waiting for the senior police officer to come down. I knew instantly, when the charge was levelled, what the repercussions of a crime like that were. I remember saying to that officer, "This man is going to get twenty years for this and he didn't do it," very clearly impressing it upon him.

You have to understand that the Robbery Squad were bad in those days, they were a law unto themselves, fitting up left, right and centre. Armed robbery was at its height, so something needed to be done. But these guys were very, very sharp and ruthless.

George hadn't been mini-cabbing long, and he was in Devons Road that day. He took some fish to a restaurant in Chancery Lane. Can you imagine at that time, ten o'clock in the morning, going along with the traffic? But the police timed it and said he could have got from Chancery Lane to Ilford by the time the robbery was committed. I mean come on, he'd have to be doing a hundred miles an hour!

Peter said, "We can't leave him in there roasting." What makes what Peter did even more incredible is that he didn't really know George. It wasn't as if they were staunch mates.

The first time I ever really met Peter and his wife Shirley – before George was arrested or anything like that – was at a friend of ours' pub, the Dover Castle, off Commercial Road. There was a party over at Canning Town, I don't know whose house it was, and I happened to get in the car with Peter and Shirley. When I got talking to Shirley, I found out they'd lost their first baby to spina bifida. I think he was about eighteen months old. Isn't that weird? I find it really strange that we should all have lost children in that way.

PETER
Shirley's relationship with those girls was one of respect. They were hard-working girls. Jeannie Ishmail and Rosie Davis kept their homes absolutely spotless. Their children were a credit to them, and they worked very, very hard. Shirley was just the same. She looked after me, she brought up five children. An absolute diamond. Proper working-class girls. Any man would be proud of them.

I think George and Rose were probably like most working-class couples. There seemed to be respect, but George was always at the bar with Mickey and the girls would always be on their own. That's how it is up and down the country in

working-class and middle-class areas: the blokes are on their
own and the women are in the corner somewhere. But I
thought they were a lovely couple, and I really liked George.

Every day Peter took me to that prison, apart from
Saturdays. Never let me down once. Monday to Friday,
Peter would pull up, and it's a hard slog from the East End
to Brixton, especially at nine o'clock in the morning with all
the traffic.

We'd get their dinner[6] and their clean clothes and all that,
and then you'd be thinking as you came out of there about
what you were going to do tomorrow. Your mind was doing
overtime. And I was ducking and diving with work; if I
could get a cash-in-hand job, I'd do it.

George was remanded to Brixton. It opened my eyes,
visiting prisons. I saw the other side of the coin, what it does
to people, how it breaks up homes. You'd see a bloke with
his wife, then you'd go on another visit and he'd be with his
girlfriend. I used to think, "Am I seeing things?" George
would say, "That's none of our business!" But I used to wind
myself up. His poor wife was probably at home, looking
after all the kids, while he was being visited by his trollop. I
used to say it out loud. He'd go, "Leave it out!" But no, I'd
want to say something.

The campaign was formed during the time we were going
up to the court hearings. I wouldn't have sat back and done
nothing, I definitely know that. I'm not saying that it
wouldn't have gone on without him, but Peter was the force
behind it. Peter always lifted your spirits, but once he got a

---

6 *Remand prisoners' spouses were still allowed to bring in home-cooked meals*
for their partners at this time.

bee in his bonnet you could not stop him. When he said he was going to Paris, I thought, "Oh my God . . ."

He went to the Champs-Elysées. They never took any notice of him, so he got up, went and got a brick, threw it through the embassy window, walked in and said, "I did that." They put him in the nuthouse, thought he was loopy. The doctor rang us up to verify that his story was true. He was only in there a couple of days.

Peter was dedicated. He lived and breathed it, his mind would be turning over 24-7. But I think it helped Peter as well. As much as he was helping us, I think he got a lot of his frustrations out.

The things he did were unbelievable. He would have made a good leader.

PETER

Prior to taking Rosie to Scotland Yard, I'd been onto the daily papers. But everyone was saying, "This is sub judice, *nothing can be done." So on the Sunday after George is charged, I take my lorry to Fleet Street and smash it straight through the glass front entrance of the* Daily Mirror, *which is in Holborn at the time. I drove up the steps, straight through into the lobby with the truck, backed it out, drove around. I did the* Evening Standard, *the* Express *and the* Telegraph *too, it must have taken me less than an hour. I drove up Fleet Street, up the Strand, through Trafalgar Square, down the Mall, straight into Buckingham Palace gates. This was all within forty-eight hours or so of him being charged. It was during the petrol shortages in the seventies, so apart from what I had in the tank, I had a fifty-gallon drum of petrol on the back that afternoon.*

When I appeared at Middlesex Sessions for all those

offences, I can't remember the words but I know I was getting respect. They weren't coming down on me. If you were doing those things today it might be different, but there was some respect for me amongst the judiciary. I had the high moral ground. I knew he didn't do it and that's what I was fighting for. They didn't have one shred of forensic evidence against him. All they had was five police officers and a woman who didn't pick him out on an ID parade, but picked him out when they went to the Old Bailey.

It was totally spontaneous and it was instant. There was no conspiracy, no planning or anything like that. I knew what was on the cards here. I knew I'd get people behind me. I did a lot of things prior to him being convicted. I threw my bike over the counter at Limehouse police station. I went to France, but it was really a farce because I smashed the British Embassy up with bricks. The embassy refused to play along – by which I mean they wouldn't nick me, which is what I was after. The police turned up and took me to the station. They released me because they weren't going to put me on a charge. I went straight back there, laid down in the traffic. Got picked up again. Straight down to the station again. It was like these police stations in America where it's all open plan. After a couple of times, the French police were going, "Encore, Peter, encore!" and clapping.

Anyway, after three or four times they were finally advised by the British Consul, under pressure from the police, that I was a lunatic and they should get me looked at. So they took me to this big jail overlooking the Seine. They took me up into the hospital wing, I was seen by a couple of psychiatrists during the night. It was quite a frightening experience in the sense that you didn't see any other inmates or guards or anything. As we were coming out of the lift, I remember looking in this room where there was a clothes rack with all these fucking straitjackets hanging up at one end.

They took me along a corridor with windows all the way along it and individual rooms, but all the windows had shutters on them. They put me into one of these rooms where there were four beds, with one French prisoner in there. You couldn't see out because of these electric shutters, so it was totally isolated. All I had in the room was this Frenchman – the poor sod was definitely off his head. If you wanted to go to the toilet there was a washing bowl there. He just used to get out of bed and go shit in the corner.

I had these interviews during the night. At the last one the doctor said to me, "Pierre, there's nothing wrong with you . . ."

"I know there's nothing wrong with me!"

"My wishes go with you. But the British Embassy told us that you were mad, and that we should look at you."

So they took me back to the police station the next morning and obviously they'd decided to deport me. These two young French detectives took me to the Garde du Nord, gave me a slap-up breakfast with a big carafe of wine. Lovely blokes they were. Then they put me on the train, and by this time I was beginning to wilt, simply because of this experience in the nuthouse. It threw me a bit. So I thought, "Get on the fucking train, get back, try Plan B." This wasn't working.

To sit in a court day after day after day is mind-blowing. It's all so stressful and you've still got a home to run, you've still got the shopping to get and the kids to see to. Apart from getting things rolling in the campaign, I was going to

Brixton every day, Monday to Friday. Saturday was the only day I had off, when his mum and dad used to go.

Jeannie Ishmail educated me about the criminal world. She was what I would call a typical gangster's moll, she loved it. She loved being in court, she loved walking in. It wasn't for me, I used to feel ashamed. But that was her personality, I'm not condemning her for it. She loved that way of life, as some girls do.

I got her jobs, money in her hand. I don't think she'd ever worked. I tried to help her as much as I could, but there was no thanks for it. She wasn't a morning person but Peter was staunch. That fellah would be round every morning to take us to Brixton, and we'd always have to wait for Jeannie. At that time I was working in Plantation House and signing in a different name, because I was getting money in my hand. She knew I had to be in work by a certain time but she was always late. She'd get in the van with the hump, then she'd sort of come out of it halfway there. I used to think, "Oh blimey, what's the matter with her?", then I started ignoring it. She used to say to me, "Pete ain't doing this for Mickey, he's doing this for Georgie."

I'd cook all our dinners on a Sunday and she'd do the dinners for the prison, and we'd reverse it the following week, so we each got a Sunday off. That was hard work – getting up at half past six on a Sunday to cook a dinner when you perhaps didn't get in till twelve, or half past twelve, after being at work. It took its toll really.

Whoever we were taking the dinner in for, they'd always find some other poor sod whose wife couldn't get up with their dinner, so we'd be cooking other dinners as well. When we went on a Friday, we'd fetch all the plates home to do their dinner on Sunday. And if you didn't get it in there by eleven, then you'd had it. We did that for about eight months.

One time I was waiting down the shop and this woman came out. "Rose, the shop don't open till half-eight on a Sunday!" I said, "I know, I put the dinner on and I forgot the peas." She must have thought, "What is she talking about? Eight o'clock on a Sunday morning?" But I'm doing dinner because I know I've got to get it to the prison by eleven. The times I ran up there and nearly dropped all the gravy. Then you'd go in on the Monday to visit, because you couldn't visit on a Sunday.

"How many potatoes did you put on? I'm sure they nicked some potatoes off."

He said the screws were nicking them. I said, "I ain't going to start counting fucking potatoes an' all!"

Then on a Monday we had to pay for all their newspapers. I made sure they got their papers in. They were very well looked after, actually. They had more than what we had, when I think about it now, though I made sure my kids didn't go short of anything.

Deana didn't like visiting the prison, but obviously she went. I used to take Rick about once a month. It was eye-opening to a kid, especially with him being in top-security.

I wasn't paying much attention to Rick and he really needed it, he was at a funny age. My daughter was sixteen, she wasn't a baby, but I shall never really know the impact it had on her. Never.

4

INNOCENT
– OK?

Peter and I used to have stand-up rows. He thought he was right, and I thought I was right. Nine out of ten times he won. When he voiced an opinion he stuck to it. I'd say to Peter, "Oh, don't do that!" He used to say, "I can't rest, I can't rest . . ."

PETER

When I made a mate, I made a mate. That's the sort of bloke I am. Once I click with somebody, I look after them, I'd do anything for them. And I really did think a lot of George, I thought he was a lovely fellah, he had a nice family and Rosie was a nice girl. I was just a good mate of his. I don't think it was the same the other way around.

But it absolutely consumed me. From day one there was nothing else on my mind except getting him released. I can honestly say that, apart from one moment in Walton jail, I never, ever doubted what I was going to do. And nobody else believed me, apart from my supporters in the campaign.

The crooks didn't believe me. It must have been a bit of a joke to them, all banged up in Brixton Prison with all the

71

*other robbers, they must have had a bit of a laugh about it.
They thought I was just some sort of a do-gooder, but I was
on a fucking mission, mate. I was naïve perhaps in the sense
that I had a strong belief in British justice. (I don't now.) My
whole strategy was to do these things and let people know
that I was ready to take the can.*

*It was the Christmas of '74 when I blew all the lights on
the Christmas tree in Trafalgar Square. I had to walk all the
way across the square to this embassy to tell the copper that
I'd done it. They were all standing there and nobody was
taking a fucking blind bit of notice of me.*

Before Peter did the Christmas tree lights on Christmas Eve,
I said, "Oh Pete, don't do that, love! Kids love Christmas."
His kids were only little. Mine were growing up.

He said, "I can't bear to think he's in there, and he should
be out here with his family." So he went to Trafalgar
Square, broke the lights, went over to a copper and said, "I
just did that."

"Fuck off and tell him over there," said the copper, "I'm
off-duty in five minutes."

We did laugh.

Everyone gave up their Christmas Day. Peter made us
march down to Scotland Yard on Christmas Eve, then we sat
outside in a van all done out with chains. I had a sore throat
or something, so I went in the chemist's facing Scotland Yard.

The lady who cleaned in there came out and gave me her
wage packet. She said, "I admire what you're doing. There
ain't a lot in there, but I'd like you to have it."

"Cor blimey!" said Peter.

I suppose we'd been there a couple of hours and this
Jewish man pulled up. He had a great big bowl of soup. "I

admire you what you're doing," he said. It all gave you a boost, you thought, "Well, not everyone's against us."

We parked right near St James's tube, I don't imagine you'd be able to do it now. We had a turkey, we had drink, we even had a Father Christmas turn up. I took my leaflets over to Westminster Cathedral when they were having their carol singing. We stood on the corner and then marched around for a while. Though there wasn't a lot of people about, there were cars going by beeping their hooters.

On Christmas morning this old tramp came along. We gave him a drink. "God bless you!" I suppose an hour went by and he brought some of his mates back. We fed them, gave them soup. I said to Peter, "It's opened my eyes how many people walk around with nowhere to go" – not only at Christmas, at anytime. That's why I always said to my kids, never laugh at an old tramp – you never know what's happened in his life.

We left there Boxing Day lunchtime. I ran round to see if the kids were alright, they were at my mother-in-law's. And my mother-in-law said, "Some people have been on the radio wishing you a Merry Christmas – they'd heard about you outside Scotland Yard."

We went to Horseferry Road Magistrate's Court on Boxing Day, or the day after. I've put on a little hat and scarf and I'm sitting in court with two well-spoken ladies sat next to me.

"What's the next case?"

"Oh, it's that nutcase Peter Chappell."

I spoke up. "I beg your pardon! How dare you say that? He's no nutcase!"

I'd already said to the solicitor that I'd like to get up and talk on his behalf. I told the magistrate that I felt responsible. He was leaving his wife and kids at home and doing it for the cause. He let him go home, which was lucky really. I think he'd got a suspended sentence on top of a suspended sentence, which was rare.

Peter was the be-all and end-all of the campaign really. My brother Colin was equally as game, but we'd have meetings: "What are we gonna do next? Come on, someone's got to come up with some ideas!" I don't know who thought of the painting on the wall – Peter thought of 'OK'. Once again, I was naïve; I thought, "What's OK sauce got to do with it?"

PETER

I remember I had a meeting with Rosie's family. I took her around to her sister's place and met some of the brothers, it was a big family. They'd obviously heard bits and pieces from Rosie about the things I'd been doing, and they came on board. I didn't know how to run a campaign, I knew nothing. I didn't have a political bone in my body up until this time. I was just a working man doing my own thing, and doing very well.

But Rosie's family must have been impressed, because whenever I asked them to jump, they jumped. They were totally one hundred percent behind me. I think it was early '75 when I got the family on board. But up until that point it had been individual actions of my own, and a bit of painting and sloganeering.

Colin was a big individual. All of that family were larger than life. He was a nice bloke, but difficult to work with because he had his own mind. I can remember when we first went out sloganeering, doing the paint. I'd been doing it for some time, but when I took him along I was putting up

'George Davis Is Innocent OK'. He took offence at that, he didn't want to offend anybody. It was too sharp, a bit too radical for him.

When I used to go to Scotland we'd see these slogans all over the place, in the toilets and all that. There were these gangs, and when they put a statement on the wall anywhere they'd always finish it off with an 'OK'. I knew what it meant, they were declaring something. There was no opinion on it, they were saying: "That's what it fucking is, okay?" So there was a difference between my slogans and Colin's slogans, but he did a lot over south London. He was great but he was difficult to work with.

I always put them in easy places. You could see them going down the road, or when you came out of a tunnel. On the railway arches at Bow Common Lane, 'G. Davis Is Innocent' is still there today.

RICK

I got used to seeing my dad's name after a while. You saw it every day, you kind of got blasé about it. It doesn't really affect you after a little while. But you can still see it, it's still on two of the bridges now, Bow Common Lane and Salmon Lane. It's the oldest graffiti in London. It doesn't really make me feel anything, it's just part of my life.

My Deana wasn't like me. I had both her and Rick in hospital with asthma at the same time as I had him in Brixton. Touch wood, Rick's not as bad now. But my girl had it all her life.

I kept it all in. Went and visited him in Brixton, did a day's work and then went up the hospital. I had her in an oxygen tent in one ward and my boy in another ward. But I never told George. I told him eventually, when they were alright, but not at the time, he couldn't have taken it. Looking back now, perhaps I should have given him a bit of worry.

He never saw any of that side of it. In his letters it was, "Can you get me this? Could you go round here? Oh, I'm shattered . . ."

I laughed. Shattered? I used to go to bed at bloody one or two o'clock in the morning and be up again at half past six, ready to go. It's got to come out somehow, hasn't it, all your pent-up anxiety? If I took the kids to the doctor's my doctor used to say to me, "I don't know how you do it." He knew all about it, obviously. "I can give you some Valium."

"No, I don't want no Valium." I've never lived on tablets.

I actually got in the nick with a knife down my zip-up boot. It was only a little pallet knife, nothing much. I wanted to prove that I could do it, as it was at the time the Price sisters were in there.[1] Top security? It was laughable.

You got to know the screws when you'd been going there for months – not to sit and talk with them personally, but they would say, "Good morning," and give the kids sweets. I'd be polite back, they were only doing a job.

When you went into top security you went through the main gates and then another lot of gates and you were in a kind of little wooden hut. When you walked in there they put the metal detector over you.

So I knew what I was going to do. I didn't even tell

---

1 *Dolours and Marian Price, both in their early twenties, were convicted for their part in the IRA's 1973 mainland bombing campaign, which injured two hundred people at the Old Bailey and Whitehall. In a rare move by the authorities, from late '73 through 1974 they were the only female prisoners at HMP Brixton, during which time they were force-fed while on hunger strike.*

Jeannie Ishmail, I kept it all to myself. She was in front and I went, "Oh, I do feel funny." The screw said, "Sit down, you've gone a terrible colour. Do you want a drop of water?" Of course he forgot about checking me.

So I got in there and came out again with that knife. I amazed myself. I dread to think what would have happened if I'd been caught with it, they'd probably have thrown me in jail.

I never told a soul, only this reporter Pat Cross. I said to him, "Don't dare let anyone know I'm doing this!" He kept his word. Jeannie said to me afterwards, "What's he come out here for?"

"He wants me to ask him some questions." I did it for a bet with him, but he never used the story.

GEORGE

We got nicked in May 1974. Our trial started the following January, which wasn't bad really, because some of them on remand had been there a lot longer than us. There's now five of us in there. Jimmy Drysdale has been nicked for receiving money from the Walthamstow Guardian, *because Mick and George England are now nicked for that as well as the Ilford robbery. This was to muddy the waters.*

The wonderful part about it was that they took money from the safe in Jimmy's pub. The bank tellers used to write on bank notes then, so they were identified. This woman teller identified the notes as coming from the bank where the money was held for the Walthamstow Guardian. *But the note that she identified was never in the wage packets – if it was a tenner, then there were no tenners in the packets.*

So that was it, Jimmy Drysdale was out of it. Unbelievable. Mickey Ishmail got picked out on the

Walthamstow job by an American woman. He had to say, "Put your hands up!" or something stupid. And she went, "I recognise his voice."

Then, when we were on trial, this woman Mrs Bone said she'd recognised me on the ID parade, but she didn't pick me out because she was frightened. Bear in mind that there were Old Bill all around her, but she was frightened. She picked me out at trial.

George England could have stopped it. She'd ID'd George, but she was now saying it was me. His barrister wanted her to say it because it cleared George, which you can understand. Me, Mick and Tommy Hole were on the A list, George was just going to get another little ten-month behind the door, that was all.

Mrs Bone from Barkingside was as blind as a bat. They proved that about dear Mrs Bone. Yet she said it was George and they took her word for it. If you saw those photos, you might say it was him. But your head doesn't get any bigger, does it? And yet the cap looked like a ping-pong ball, he couldn't get it on his head. How did they work that one out?

GEORGE

What eventually happened was that George and Tom got acquitted. Jim got acquitted when the jury came back. Mick got a retrial, they couldn't reach a verdict on him. I got 'guilty'. Solely on the police ID and that woman.

There was nothing, no scientific evidence whatsoever. Not a hair, no saliva. There were bloodstains, but what was pointed out later was that if that blood had been available when we went up for committal, we'd probably never have got committed for trial. But they kept saying they never had the results back, and they did. It didn't match any of us. There was a woman called Dr Perera who could break it down into seven or eight different parts, but none of us had the same genetic code. (Mick had one of those obscure groups that about one in a million of the population have.)

But when the trial was on, every day seemed to go against me. Every single one of my main witnesses had form: Terry Calvey, Jimmy Murphy, Peter. I never had anyone straight up there except my brother and Rose, but they were relatives so they didn't come over. There were no independent witnesses who were straight. When they said, "Mr Chappell, you've twelve previous convictions," he said, "No I haven't, I've got thirteen."[2] Which was Peter – wallop!

I knew it had to be double figures, because of the shooting and the injuries to the two policemen. I was prepared to get a guilty, but I was absolutely in ribbons. I was shaking. I stood up in the dock and said, "I'm completely and absolutely innocent of this offence. I've told nothing but the truth. I cannot and will not accept this verdict, and I will fight in every possible way!"

They were all up in the public gallery and they all started screaming. I heard Peter: "Yeah, you won't be on your own!"

Then they said, "Clear the public gallery."

I've often thought that jury must have thought George looked the part. If he'd have been a scrawny little man sitting there, he'd never have got convicted. But he was a big man. I reckon they looked at him and thought, "I can see him being an armed robber."

---

2 *Peter Chappell's convictions stretched back more than a decade previously, since when he'd kept out of trouble.*

All those fellahs sitting in that dock had previous form. Georgie was the only one that had never been in prison. All the others got off and he got twenty years. Can you imagine that?

I think I went deaf when I heard the sentence. Matthews, the detective in charge, came out, and I remember saying to him, "You don't realise what you've started."

The first time we ever went into Wormwood Scrubs, Peter and me, it was a shock. George had just got the twenty years, and I can't describe the colour of him.

"Oh, you've got to get me out of here . . ."

He's not a little man, he's a big fellah. But this is all down to me? I've got to take it all on my shoulders?

"This'll drive me mad!"

Not how are you, how are the kids? "Oh," I used to think, "for fuck's sake, come on, show a bit of backbone."

Of course, it must have had a big impact on him. But then it did on me. It must change a person, but it was always a case of "I ain't been well!" with him.

GEORGE

I'd never been in prison, only in Brixton on remand. It suited me really – being Category A, you were in a cell on your own. But then when I got to the Scrubs, which was completely different, it started to sink in that that was your sentence.

I was in A wing originally. A couple of guys came through who were serving long sentences and I would talk to them. There were some guys over in C wing who I knew, sending me bits and pieces over which made life a bit easier. Then I moved over to C wing and there was more going on. I got a job, I went into a shop and there was a guy there who recognised me from the local papers. He told the screw who was running the shop, "He'll come and work with us." That sort of got me out of it. You weren't thinking about the sentence all the time.

The only thing when you're doing a big sentence is that you tend to be noticed by other cons, youngsters who are impressed. Why, I have no idea. But I was on the landing with these two guys who'd get my shirts ironed. They didn't have to, but they were friends. Sometimes they could get me out of a night, I'd go down and sit in their bit and have a cup of tea. So they eased me in.

In the meantime Rose was telling me about what was occurring outside with regard to marches and stuff like that. I don't think I was in there long before Pat Cross, the reporter, was putting something in the East London Advertiser *every week. It was great, even though it wasn't national press. Whatever he did, it really heartened me. And then they moved me down to Albany, on the Isle of Wight.*

PETER

The campaign didn't start to have any form or structure until I started to get posters and leaflets done, in a small way. There were lots of them, but I didn't have the ability at that time to get really big posters done, which is what we did later on. I think the first march came a week after George had been sent down, in March 1975. All the others had got off. Our first leaflet was entitled 'Who Is George Davis?' with a big question mark.

The first thing we ever did was go on the underground. We had loads of leaflets done. We met up at six o'clock at Mile End, there were about a dozen of us. At that time of the morning it's only the office cleaners on the tube. One of us had a bag of water and a sponge, the other one had all the leaflets. One wet, one stuck, and we covered the train. We caught the first train out, but we only got as far as the Bank. At Bank station, the police were waiting at all the different entrances.

I don't know whether it was Mile End station that tipped them off. But obviously they didn't know who we were, at that stage. A few of us got away, a couple of us got caught.

The funniest court I ever went to was the one at the Bank, where they still wear the traditional dress, the white tights. I've never paid the fine. Never. I won't do it on principle.

The next thing was plastering London Bridge with leaflets. A copper came up to one of them. "Stop doing that and I won't arrest you."

"Fuck off!" They still carried on and they all got nicked, all twelve of them. Some of our laws go back to the sixteenth century, litter laws and that sort of thing.

The police in general showed some tolerance of us. We did Fleet Street and Pete tied us all together with this chain, three girls weighing a total of eighteen stone. Can you imagine?

I think it was outside *The Times*. Stopped the lorry. All calm. Lifted up the back, we got out, sat down in the road. Everyone was looking this way and that. Then this copper ran at me, screaming, "Get up!"

I wasn't moving. We were holding all the traffic up. Then they sent in the black Marias. You can imagine the chain rattling as they bundled us in.

When we were in Fleet Street we'd written on the pavement, 'G. Davis Is Innocent'. But when we heard the squad car, no one had put the 's' on the end of 'Davis'. Everyone ran and hid. I don't know if it was Peter or Colin, but he went back, put the 's' on and got nicked.

They took us to Snow Hill police station. Put us in the cell but didn't lock it. One girl, a real comedienne I'm still friends with today, walked straight in and went, "I want a glass of water. I know my rights!"

The copper pissed himself laughing. One of the police came round and actually asked us how we started the campaign. He wanted to set up a campaign for the wives of police officers who had died on duty.

The City Police and the Met Police are two different forces. I didn't know that at the time. The City police were wonderful. Not like in Bethnal Green. They locked us in cells. All the women with kids came to give themselves up and they told them to piss off. As they were arguing with the police, the kids were weeing in the buckets outside the cells.

But as I've always said, I think that when the Met arrested George, Mickey and the others they genuinely thought they had the right people.

GEORGE

I'd known I was going to be convicted. I called the police in before we went to trial to ask for the A10 to come in. They were the people that looked into complaints about the police. I told them, "I'm going to get convicted for something I haven't done. I want you to look into it because there's lies being told."

"Ah well, we can't talk about that. We've got to wait until you're convicted and then you'll have to appeal."

When his appeal was refused, we were outside the court. Next door to the Law Courts were double doors, and I knew he was going to come out of there. Peter told me to lay across that. I said, "Oh Peter, it's been a long day . . ." "Lay across it!" So I did.

Of course, the van's come out and I'm laying there. They got out and lifted me up. I weighed six stone seven. And off they went. They were quite polite about it.

Looking back, I can see that something was driving us on. Adrenalin, I suppose.

Colin, my brother who we buried recently, was a diamond, as game as a beigel.[3] We took the kids to block the road across Bethnal Green. An articulated lorry came across and my Colin got under the wheels. He said to the driver, "If you move this, you'll go right over me."

"I won't move it, mate!"

He laid right under the wheels. All the kids were crying. He held the traffic up for about twenty minutes.

He stood on the dome of St. Paul's Cathedral, God rest his soul, him and my other brother, Jimmy, on a four-foot ledge for seven hours with a great big banner. That takes some guts, how many fellahs would do that? One was a builder and the other pulled them down. Colin was a demolition worker, pulled all of Gardners Corner[4] down. He had a thing for heights, but then he was in the parachute troop.

He painted an old cinema they closed down in the Old Kent Road with 'George Davis Is Innocent', all in bright-coloured paint. You couldn't help but notice it. Him and Peter did all the bridges. One held the other one upside down. I couldn't have done it, but I've seen Colin climb. They both risked their lives.

My younger brothers and my sisters all rallied round. Not

---

3 Rose uses the traditional Yiddish East End spelling and pronunciation of 'bagel'.
4 In the Whitechapel/Aldgate neighbourhood.

so much my youngest brother, David, because he wasn't that way inclined. I can remember that he was working for the council in the flats that I lived in, painting. I said to him, "We've got a big march tomorrow."

"I can't make it, I've got a bit of overtime."

I was raving. "If they're all fucking like you when we have another war, we'll have to go and bury ourselves!" Not thinking about how he had a wife and kids to worry about. I admire him for saying it now. But I didn't at the time.

I was only thinking about my own family, which is selfish really. I just thought everyone had to drop everything and be there.

George had really lovely parents, and it absolutely broke their hearts when he got that twenty years. They were different people. It was heartbreaking to see them, it really was.

They were such law-abiding citizens. His dad was a petty officer in the navy, always went to work, never a lazy man. But sometimes I would look at them and think, "I wish you had a bit more fight in you." I know that sounds horrible, and I don't mean it to be. But if that had been my son, I'd have been up in arms. "Oh, what are we going to do?" his mum would say. "What's going to happen now?"

They weren't people that would put themselves up the front, but they'd come on a march. I don't think they liked it, but they knew as parents that they had to stand by their son.

Yet he had an aunt who lived on my landing, my mother-in-law's sister, who was like a mum to me. You could *not* have the hump around her because she was so funny, everyone loved her. If I was short on money I could go along to her and she'd always lend me a tenner. (I always paid her back.)

She had more go in her than any man I knew. Her name

was Joanna, 'Aunt Jo'. She was married to one of the Readings from Canning Town, a big family, all wheelers and dealers. Her husband used to be a bare-fist fighter, 'Punched-Up Nose Albert'. Her and Ann, my mother-in-law, were sisters, but you would never have put them together. Ann was very quiet, but Jo was very loud.

You couldn't frighten her. When the television licence first came out, they knocked at my door and we got done, we never had a licence. So when they'd gone we rang Aunt Jo: "The television people are round, they're picking you at random."

"Oh, let them knock, I'll tell them I ain't got one."

So the husband said, "They'd say, 'What's that, a mirage?'"

"So I'd say, 'No, it ain't working.'"

"What would you say about that aerial up on the wall?" It was one of those old-fashioned telly aerials, a round thing with spikes.

"I'd say my old man's a fucking Martian!"

She'd be right behind me. She'd get on a bus with the leaflets, go to give one away and they might say no. She'd say, "No? It'll be your fucking son tomorrow!" Oh, I had to walk away. She was well into her sixties by then, and she didn't give a shit for anyone.

All the fight that my mother-in-law didn't have, she had it. She went on marches, screaming and hollering. As, to be fair, did his cousins. But I think it was all such a great shock to my mother- and father-in-law. They were devastated, they both aged overnight.

George's mum went into a decline really, but it gave Aunt Jo more energy: "No one takes the piss out of us and gets away with it!" She was behind me one hundred percent. If I had to go anywhere for a weekend with the campaign, she'd have the kids, feed them and look after them. She was a brick.

She only died a few years ago now. I got to the hospital ten minutes after. I miss her, she really was a lovely lady. But you can't live forever, can you?

RICK

She was like a third nan to me. Because she lived along the landing I was in there most of the time. All the press loved her because she'd cook dinner for them. I remember them all knocking at the door, with their highest bids for stories.

My boy could have had free school dinners when George went away, but I wouldn't have let him. I wasn't that bloody destitute. I know what it's like, they don't do it now, they do it discreetly, but years ago everyone had to put their hands up.

During the campaign I was on social security, but I was ducking and diving. I was doing jobs for money in my hand and I worked for my manageress at Plantation House. She lived down the Roman Road. She said, "Do you want to clean for me on a Saturday? I'll give you twenty-five bob."[5] Which wasn't bad. You could buy a nice bag of shopping with that. Then I'd go home, get changed, Rick would go along to Aunt Jo's and I'd go to work as a waitress at a banquet for the night.

So she gave me her keys. Rick was about nine then. "Going up that big Jean's, are we today?" I couldn't have wished for a better little boy, until he was about twelve. I'd been cleaning for her for about a year. She had a three-bedroom maisonette,

---

5 £1.25.

it was a nice place. And she'd left me a note: "Dear Rose, if you've got time could you do a bit of ironing?"

When I looked at the ironing it was from the floor to the ceiling.

I got into work. "One minute, I'll give you your money."

"No, don't bother Jean."

"Oh. Why?"

"Fucking three-bedroom maisonette? Clean it, polish it, do the floors, hoover, make the beds – then have I got any time for ironing? Stick your twenty-five bob up your arse!"

I never went there any more. She was shocked, but she was still my friend after that.

I didn't have to work like I did. If I'd have been that sort of person, my family would have supported me. My mum never had a lot, but she used to do me a nice dinner.

But I never let them know how desperate I was. That's not me. They'd have given me money every week if I'd have wanted it. But no, I've got my pride.

When you've got to, you have to. I've cleaned toilets, I've cleaned up on a building site. I'd do any variety of jobs if I needed the money.

Hard work kills no one. But worry can.

It was two years' hard slog really. And it took its toll. This was also around the very first time I ever found a lump in my breast. I neglected it, I did nothing about it.

GEORGE

I blame my solicitor for quite a lot of what had happened. I'd said to him, "You've got to go and see these people," who I'd been driving the minicab for, "because they're witnesses but they don't know me. You've got to go and remind them." So what did they do? I think we were committed in August, I'd been in the cells since May. They put in a notice of alibi with all these people's names on. Of course, when he didn't call them the prosecution were saying, "Where are these witnesses? This is your notice of alibi, you haven't called them." He said he couldn't call them because they didn't know who I was – it would have been like calling any stranger. It was ridiculous. I ran my solicitor down, bitterly, at every opportunity.

We went and painted the Middle Temple and they never ever questioned it. We wrote, 'Jimmy Stephenson is the bentest solicitor around here' in bright yellow paint, all along the walls and pavements. No one complained.

He was our solicitor, and he most probably wasn't bent, but he wasn't doing half of what he said he was. I was finding out more than he was. I went to Lord Soper and Lord Longford, who was actually a really nice man and did a lot for us.

So did Robert Kilroy-Silk, who was an MP for West Ham at the time. He was very outspoken, he didn't beat about the bush: "What made you think your husband is innocent?" He wrote letters on our behalf. The local reporter, Pat Cross, used to get pulled in by the editor: "You can't put this in!" But he always managed to get something in the *East London Advertiser*. Even Bill Oddie sent me £50.

PETER

Rosie was an honest, working-class woman. All her family were honest. They all worked, none of them were villains, none of them were crooks, they worked fucking hard in demolition and things like that. What little she knew about the other side of life was because she'd been dragged into it by George's relationship with Ishmail and her connection with Jeannie. She was dragged into their sphere. So what I learned very early on in that campaign was never to push myself forward but to always push Rosie, taking her to places, putting her upfront. I wanted her to be seen by the public. I wanted the public to identify with her, and I knew they would.

I used to take her to meetings with the police when we were organising marches. I took her round to see Lord Soper. I took her to see Lord Longford. I was always pushing her forward but she wasn't political at all. Neither was I, and I treated the police courteously. (Rosie didn't go for the jugular though, whereas I always did.) I took her to meetings with the dock workers. I took her to meetings with the reporters at Smithfield, because at a certain point during that campaign I started to turn towards the unions to try to get them involved. So I was gradually politicised, and I was beginning to realise that I had to penetrate more into working-class organisations because they had the power and the means to do things. But the campaign cut right across the social strata. It was unique.

This Methodist minister named David Moore even let me paint 'George Davis Is Innocent' outside on his church board. Then he asked me to go and meet all the young men who were training to become priests that Sunday morning, and do a little thing for the radio.

This little priest said to me, "Don't you think you're using the Church?"

I said, "Well, I was brought up to believe that churches are there to be used."

It was only up on the board for two or three hours

before the board of directors told him to get it off. He had to paint over it. But we had people like him, a militant vicar, helping us.

But then you had the piss-takers. "Oh it's them again, the George Davis campaign!"

I went to the Home Office and demanded to see someone, with a great big clock in my bag. This was when the bombs were going off. They couldn't nick me for having an alarm clock, could they? I made sure it was a really loud one though.

They took me in an office and this civil servant came in. I refused to leave till they'd heard me, but then there was a knock on the door

"You're wanted urgently on the phone."

"That was all planned before I came in 'ere!" I said. "Don't take me for a mug!"

If I had a fiver, I'd write 'George Davis Is Innocent' across it. (That's defacing the Queen's likeness!) They must have known it was my handwriting. Every fiver I'd got, I'd go in the shop: "Could you change that for five ones?" Every letter I wrote, I'd write it across the back of the envelope, every bit of correspondence I sent to the prison.

We did manage to have some laughs, and it was a bloody good job too. But I don't believe anything like the campaign will ever happen again.

RICK

I was only nine when the campaign got started up, still very young. My earliest memories are probably of Peter Chappell and that coming round. Everybody would sit round in our house, or go round to Aunt Jo's. Then gradually it got bigger and bigger, and the amount of people who came through the door grew until it looked like hundreds. They'd have meetings at night and there would be sixty people sometimes in the house.

I remember the marches on a Sunday, but as a child you're in a daydream really, aren't you? I can remember my mum being out a lot of the time and going with her on the marches, to hand out leaflets on the bridge. I remember going to school and everyone asking about my dad and what was happening, even the teachers knew about it, all the parents and everybody. It was kind of like mini-celebrity – not that I was Big Time Charlie, I wasn't famous, but the campaign was. Everybody in the East End knew about it.

During the campaign, when he was in prison, you'd go round to anyone's house and you were always aware that other people were talking about you without talking about you, if you know what I mean. People would assess you by it. If I was taken anywhere by my uncle, it was always, "This is George's boy."

Ordinary people got up off their arse and marched with us. People had time off work. Even when we booked the marches, the police took us all to places where no one would see us. Peter would go, "No, we ain't having that, definitely not!" I used to think, "Oh, don't upset them, Pete," but he was right. We had three marches, with pretty good turnouts.

We all met at the Tower of London. Peter got up and spoke, it was when the new bypass took you right in towards Big Ben. We marched on Saturday morning from Tower Hill to Whitehall, in the spring of 1975. But you walk through the City of a weekend and there's no one around. We were marching with no one there.

We had to chant, "What do we want? Justice! Who for?

George Davis!" from start to finish, with Peter on a loudspeaker.

Where we'd been up the night before until the early hours of the morning, someone forgot to put the 'e' at the end of 'George' on our banner.

"Can't you even spell 'George'?" called out this kid from a coach.

"We left it," I said, "so that people like you would look at it!" But we hadn't, we were so tired that we'd forgotten it.

My mum made her own way to Downing Street and stood at the gates. She was a big woman, she was only short but she had big boobs. (Well, she'd had twelve kids!) We'd had T-shirts made up with 'George Davis Is Innocent', but half of it went under her arms.

My mum was proud of what we were doing, but that was a big part of her, she was gutsy: "Go on, girl, let them have it!"

I know it affected my daughter. She wasn't a loud girl, Deana, but she went even more into her shell. I took her and my son with me to hand in our petition at Downing Street, and she was cringing. "Oh Mum, I don't want to do it." And I'd say, "Well, it's for your father." I kind of forced her.

She wouldn't sit in on any meetings or anything, she always went up to her bedroom. We've got film of Rick, who was only a little boy, walking on the marches with his head up. But Deana was very shy.

PETER

The real breakthrough came when I organised a march from Tower Hill to 10 Downing Street via Westminster Bridge, Trafalgar Square, the Cenotaph and Whitehall. A chap called Martin Walker found one of our leaflets that day and

26 APR 1975

C/26
4.

23-4-75

Dear Davis,
59 Belton Way,
Bow London E.3.

Dear Dad

Hope you're feeling alright
I'm sorry I never writ last week
only there wasn't much to tell
you, This week we went and
sat in the middle of Fleet
St Protesting, and the Police
thought we were Womens's
Libbers until we gave them
a leaflet (Justice for Davis),
Oh I know what I want to ask
you dad as you know
Nanny and Granddad were

To

Mr George Davis, 131890,
H.M. PRISON,
WORMWOOD SCRUBS,
Du Care R.D,
P.O Box 757,
London W.12.

3/69

BOW
10-AM
24 APR
1975
E.3

REMEMBER
to use
POST CODE!

7½

very upset when this happened and there longing to see you so I was wondering could you send them a visiting order, also dad I know mummy's always going on about Big Ricky but he does care about you and the only reason he doesn't come round or phone up is because mummy would insult him anyway I hope you understand dad.

I must say you looked really great when I saw you the other week I almost fancied you myself (chatta ha ha)

everyone here sends their

love dad especially me and little Rick, mummys fighting really hard to get you home dad and I know in the end she'll win anyway dad keep you're head high love and miss you very much

Deana
&
xx xxxxx Ricky xxx

P.S
Remember dad
Justice for Davis

contacted me, because it was always my phone number at the bottom of these leaflets. He became a real servant of the campaign, one of the rocks that I rested on, especially when I was inside – him and another chap called Ian Cameron.

Ian used to work for Up Against The Law, and did an examination of the evidence against George Davis that, even to this day, is the best work on the subject. It really put it under a microscope. I'm not absolutely sure how I first came across him, but I do remember going to the premises that Up Against the Law were operating out of in Kings Cross one evening. Ian showed me their magazine, UPAL, which I think he edited at the time. Him and his friends all came out of the 1968 upheavals, the Angry Brigade, the American Embassy, Vietnam and all that. But what impressed me about both of those guys is they didn't try to take over at all. Martin was a student at the North London Poly when they had a big sit-in there, an occupation, which went on for weeks. He was radicalised by that. He was also an artist at the time, a poster designer.

I went to Martin and asked him if he could design a poster based on a particular march or demonstration of ours. As Banksy recognises,[6] we were quite sophisticated in a way, with our slogans and the way that we were developing ourselves. We were certainly not political, but we were a group of people struggling with a problem. I've always found that when you get into a struggle, you find the words and means to articulate it. I'm a strong believer in struggle developing people. If you had a young child with a terrible affliction, for instance, then because of the struggle of

---

6 *For his legendary graffito, Peter Chappell is credited as 'Graffiti Hero #3' on the guerrilla artist's* Banksy Manifesto *website.*

looking after that child you'd become conscious of something that you weren't previously aware of.

The beauty of that campaign was that it was working class, we had total control of it. There were no politicos involved, we were the guv'nors. Lefties and educated people all got involved, but they worked with us, they took our orders. We didn't have the SWP or any of those fucking tossers coming along and trying to take over.

GEORGE

It absolutely keeps you going. When the national press start picking it up then it's big time. There was one guy in there, I never even spoke to him, in fact I didn't like him one iota, but he would say to someone else, "I found something in here for George." I thought, bollocks, give it back to him.

But the fact that Up Against The Law were doing all that stuff meant I was the lucky one. They did it for a lot of people, but it certainly made you feel a lot better knowing that those people were out there.

We picketed ITV and marched outside there. Little David Hamilton looked at a few of the signs and looked down his nose at us. I said, "It might be you one day!" Sir Richard Attenborough was the same.[7]

But when I stood outside Whitechapel station at a table with petitions, people on the whole were pretty supportive. They were East Enders then, people united. I don't think they would do it today.

---

7 *Attenborough played the serial killer Christie in the 1970 film of Ludovic Kennedy's* Ten Rillington Place. *The basis of Kennedy's study is the grave injustice done to Timothy Evans, wrongfully convicted and subsequently hanged.*

You might get the odd little street like where I live. I've got lovely neighbours, but they're unique now, a one-off. Years ago all the streets were like that. The City's moving more and more into the East End and they're taking it over. There won't be any East End soon.

People used to write loads of letters to the campaign. We had nasty ones too – I had a packet of shit put through the letterbox. The postman put it through in a proper envelope. I looked at it and said, "Everyone shits on me." The postman laughed, and so did I. I went and put it down the chute.

Then you got the cranks who wrote, "You should rot in Hell." They all came out of the woodwork.

RICK

We'd go down the Lane and hand out leaflets to people. Some people would throw them back at you. Even as a kid, you'd start having a go back at them for not believing him. We'd have lunatics ring up, because the posters had our phone number on it: "I'm going to kill your dad. I'm going to come round and kill you . . ." And this is on the end of the phone. We had one nutter who'd just ring up in the middle of the night. It was proper frightening, some of it.

But there were more decent letters. The sad thing is that a lot of them were from mothers whose sons were in prison, but I had too much going on in the campaign already. I know it helped a lot of people and gave a lot of encouragement. I think we proved one thing, that there is power in numbers.

But you only have to look back at the industrial strikes and then look at the scabs. I can see their point of view,

although I'd never be a scab. They've got kids and a wife. So do you let them suffer or do you only look after your own?

I also learned at the time not to always believe what you read in the papers. They came and took me to France to

---

8 *Recent forensic reinvestigations have suggested that human remains buried in the cellar of Hawley Harvey Crippen's Camden home may have been male. This would undermine his 1910 conviction and execution for the murder of his wife, and possibly lend credence to his claim that the burial must have predated his residency. The evidence is far from conclusive, but it remains a possibility that Dr Crippen was indeed innocent.*

meet with Ben, a young bloke who'd been working for the minicab firm when George delivered the fish that morning. They said I'd be back that same day, but I wasn't. Given how people fleece the papers, I could have taken them for some new night clothes, but I didn't.

The reporter took me to a beautiful hotel. It was his birthday and I watched him stand and get pissed. Brandy after brandy, then a coffee, then a brandy. And the next morning the paper read: "Rose runs along the quayside to meet Ben . . ."

I said to him, "That's a lie!" "Well, that's what we have to do," he said.

Poor Ben was an illegal immigrant. He went to France because he was frightened they were going to chuck him back to wherever he came from. He was quite a nice man. He actually came back and married an Englishwoman to stay in this country. I even went to his wedding!

PETER

Sometimes my cases went to the Crown Court. But because this was all happening within quite a short period these things were mounting up, and it was only after Headingley, where I was at Crown Court again, that they were all taken into consideration. But there were times during the campaign when I was imprisoned for short periods for contempt of court. I took the girls up to Bethnal Green, where they sat down in the middle of the street and were arrested. My Shirley was done for assaulting a copper – absolute fucking nonsense! So I was in the back of the court there that day, and I shouted out, "It's a bleeding kangaroo court!" My Shirley would never do a thing like that. She's a working-class mother, never been in trouble in her fucking life!

So I was jailed there. And when this occurred during the early months of the campaign, as soon as they put me in prison I'd go on hunger strike. The longest was for about twenty-three days, there was another one at seventeen. There were three different hunger strikes before I was released. No water and no bread, nothing at all.

Lord Gifford got me released pending appeal from the last stretch, at Pentonville, after twenty-three days. I was in a fucking bad state. They sent a vicar in to me every day, trying to get me off it, but I wasn't having it. I recovered immediately as soon as I got out and started eating. But my thoughts on those sorts of tactics have changed since those days, because those are desperation stakes. What you're saying really is that you've got nothing else left to give. It's too extreme. There's something wrong with your campaign if you have to resort to that. But those were times when I was running out of ideas, though not running out of support. It hadn't really started to come together.

All those things were hushed up by Fleet Street. There were just little bits in the paper, not really having an effect. But when we did the Headingley thing, they all came into play. People realised then that this campaign had been going on for some time and it gathered force. It just brought it all together.

During that summer I'd been imprisoned in Pentonville on hunger strike. All I was doing was living for that campaign. The vicar said to me, "During a lull, try to find something else to do." So when I came out, there was about an acre of waste ground where I was living. Me and this ex-docker organised all the kids on the estate to clear it, and we eventually made an adventure playground out of it during the summer holidays. From toddlers to fifteen-year-olds, they spent their whole day from early in the morning to late at night with us on that piece of poxy ground. They'd come out of a morning scrubbed and go home at night fucking black as the ace of spades, absolutely rotten. They worked like little Trojans all day long.

I remember working on this playground as the final Test match started, I think it was on a Friday. I'd been thinking about an idea that had just started to grow in my brain. It was really spontaneous and it had formed by the Sunday. I contacted one person, they contacted someone else, then they contacted someone else. In the end I had Colin, Richard Ramsey, who was a nephew of Rosie's, and Geri Hughes, an American woman. I just told them there and then, "We're going to go up north and stop this cricket match."

The beauty of it was that it was the fifth and final Test. The Aussies already held the Ashes, this series was to decide who would take over the Ashes this year. When we went out on the Sunday, by the Monday I think England had batted and at the end of that day it was really finely balanced. Australia had to bat the next day, but England were definitely in with a chance of spinning them out.

We arrived there on the Monday morning and decided that we'd send Colin and Richard into the ground that day just to reconnoitre. I would reconnoitre the outside with Geri. Outside the ground there was this high wall that went all the way around. At the back there was a high wall on the left-hand side and on your right were the back gardens of these nice, well-to-do houses. There was an alleyway that ran in between the wall and those back houses, and at various points along the alleyway were lampposts, six inches away from the wall.

So it was very simple: a man could just climb up the lamppost and he was in the ground. We decided that me and Colin would go into the ground, while Richard and Geri would paint the slogans outside the front gate. But, to kill some time, we left Leeds and went to a motorway station for a cup of tea and a bite to eat.

I didn't know that much about cricket, so when I actually arrived that night I found the ground was like concrete, not grass. There was no softness there, it was fucking rock hard. We needed tools to do that but we didn't have them at the time. We took some metal knives and things from the motorway café, but I had a brainwave and thought that, as well as digging the pitch up, I'd take a gallon of oil down there and spread some at each end of the pitch, just by the crease where the bowler puts his arms over – the area where he needs to have sure footing.

As Colin and me climbed up over the wall, it was all dark and you could see out onto the middle of the pitch. The covers were over the pitch itself. I took one end, Colin took the other and we got under the covers without being noticed. I dug some little holes up the best I could, and then spread the oil around where the bowler comes in. We did our business, came out from under the covers in the half-light, ran across the pitch, climbed up the wall and down the other side. Everything went perfectly. Round the front of the stadium Richard and Geri had done their job, no problems at all. We got in the car, bang, straight down to London. Everything went off swimmingly. It ended like an SAS operation.

RICK

Probably the event that sticks in my mind is Headingley. That was really the biggest one that I can remember. It was a lovely hot day, and I was taken round to my aunt's in Stratford because my mum had gone away. They'd gone down to Leeds, my mum and Richie, my Aunt Chris's husband. We all knew that they'd done it. Then all of a sudden it was on the television, with the realisation that George Davis was really going to come to the front. People were going to notice more about what was happening to him.

PETER

I think we arrived in London about six o'clock on the Tuesday morning. I went straight to bed, but I've got to confess I didn't know at the time just how reactionary the cricket authorities and the Establishment would be – in particular Rees-Mogg, who was the editor of The Times. The immediate reaction in the papers that day was so fucking over-the-top it was absolutely spot on, just what I wanted. One Australian reporter actually asked, "Can they hang these people for this?" They just played right into our hands. Even in the prison system at the time, as George will tell you, there were fucking ructions. Then they realised who it was, and it was, "Go on lads!"

I couldn't imagine that, when I woke up, there would be maybe three to five hundred reporters outside my house. But I slipped into gear. I took cups of tea out to them, keeping everything close to my chest, not answering any questions. I was at the centre of the campaign and had been through it all, whereas Colin, Richard and Geri weren't as experienced at handling the media. The reporters got hold of Colin and got him pissed, and Geri started talking too. I'm not criticising those two people because we weren't properly prepared. That was the beauty of our campaign, we just didn't stop fighting even though we were making mistakes all the time.

The reporters were encamped outside my house for a few days. On the second or third day these four coppers from Yorkshire came down. There were all these crowds of reporters outside, plus all the kids that I'd been working with, it was like a carnival. I'm sitting chatting with these reporters, always careful not to talk about what we'd done.

The coppers go to knock on the door and I'm outside with the reporters, just sitting on the wall. I was making fools of them but that wasn't what it was about. I wasn't about to portray myself in the media as taking the piss out of them.

So I went over to the door as Shirley was talking to them. Shirley said, "I don't know where he is," and they were beginning to walk away. But I went over and pulled them back.

"Can I help you?"

"Are you Peter Chappell?"

"Yeah."

"Can we have a word with you?"

"Of course you can."

"Can we go inside?"

"No. If you're going to have a word with me, I need these people here." The BBC and ITV were there with their cameras.

One of the things that was driving the campaign right from the very beginning was keeping a spotlight on the police. So this was part of that, if I'm going to have any talks with the police I want witnesses. They said okay, went off in their car and disappeared.

The next thing, I was hearing it from the wireless, the telly and the papers that Colin and Geri were talking a lot, and things were getting a bit out of control. Because at that point I'd been prepared to deny everything and go for trial.

But because things were getting out of hand, I phoned this Yorkshire copper up and said, "I'm coming down to talk to you." I went down to New Scotland Yard and made a statement to say that I dug the pitch up. I didn't give any names but I told them how it was done. When the news got out that I'd given myself up, Geri, Colin and Richard all did the same thing.

That put a stop to some of the things that were happening previously. Certain elements in the media knew there was a big story in this, and they were plying Colin with drink. Rest his soul, he went over to Victoria Park and started taking up the cudgels on behalf of this poor mental patient who had flipped his lid and was on the island in the lake. The police went over there and dragged him off the island, and he was dead when they got him back to the police station. There was quite a bit of that in the East End. Colin decided to publicise that by stripping bollock-naked, running over to the island and prancing about. I was just involved in getting George out of prison, I didn't need this. So that is why I gave myself up. We weren't the be-all and end-all of campaigns, we weren't fucking fighting for everybody, just George Davis!

Colin went over Vicky Park, stripped off naked and got a rowing boat. Then you saw two policemen in a rowing boat trying to catch him up. He got to the middle of the island and climbed a tree. "You want me, you come and get me!" Even the police were laughing, it was hilarious. Then he got dressed and the police brought him back in his 'Free George Davis' shirt. He didn't give a monkey's. But it got in the paper.

PETER

Richard was stonewalling them all, but Geri and Colin were just talking too much. There only needed to be one person speaking to the media about it, and that was me. I'd have answered all the questions and I wouldn't have admitted to anything. I'd have gone to trial on it. But because of all the statements they were making, it was unlikely that we'd get away with it. If they'd not said a word we could have had a really good trial, a cracker.

Mike Mansfield[9] said to me afterwards, "Why did you plead guilty?" I just wanted to put a stop to all the shenanigans. We had a job to do, we did the job, now this was the time to take it onto the next step.

It was Peter's idea about the cricket. My Colin played cricket and his son recently played at Lords. My nephew is a brilliant cricketer. But Colin said it in a telly interview: "It broke my heart to dig that pitch up, because I love cricket. And we looked like winning the Ashes, didn't we? But what's a bit of dirt to a man's life?" Which is true, isn't it? People should have got their priorities right.

Aunt Jo's son-in-law went with them to do the pitch. He'd never been in trouble. Richie went to give himself up when he heard all the others had. I knew it was going to happen, but I couldn't get my head around it. I said, "What difference is digging up a fucking bit of dirt going to

---

9 Michael Mansfield QC is indelibly identified as the anti-Establishment silk. He has represented everyone from the families of slaying victims Stephen Lawrence and Jean Charles de Menezes to Mohamed Al Fayed – during the Harrods owner's conspiracy accusations against the Royal Family at the Diana inquest.

- 5 SEP 1975

In replying to this letter, please write on the envelope:—

Number 1890   Name DAVIS

H.M. PRISON,
ALBANY,
NEWPORT,
ISLE OF WIGHT

- 9 SEP 1975

Dear Rose,
                I got your letter on Thursday
but you never said when you would
be coming to see me. I got a letter
from my mum saying she would be
visiting me on Wednesday. I have been
reading the Mirror with the case in.
So you went to France and met
Ben. I am still in the dark as to
whats happening. I should have thought
Ben should have seen Wendy Mantle
and made his statement. Mr Moulder
is only supposed to be inquiring
into the police, not my alibi. Rose, I
need to see you urgently. There are
some things I want you to do, but
I will have to see you to explain
properly. I got a letter from Wendy
Mantle asking me to write to the
appeal court giving precise reason's
why I want to change solicitors.
I want you to get in touch
with her and tell her, I have

No. 243 30141 8-2-68

written to them, but the only reason I gave was that they never acted in my interest. I decided I would not go into detail with those people. If they were trying to help me, they would not need to ask stupid questions. I told them before that I am innocent and therefore I was let down. What more do they need to know. I think it is disgusting that a man cannot change his solicitor without their permission. All I want is justice and they are trying to prevent me from getting it. Anyhow Rose, as I said in my last letter, I want to know whats going on. The Guardian was talking about a bail application pending my appeal. I would like to know a bit more about that. Also what happened about those elderly women and is the fishman going to make a statement to Wendy Manila? Rose, I am going to Wendy Manila. Rose, I am going mad in here, trying to guess what is happening. I know you can't write everything in a letter, but I feel really frustrated not having... I saw in the papers that they turned down my...

Rose, surely people can see now that there is something to hide. How can three men and a woman be locked up for admitting to digging up a bit of dirt. After all, thats all it is. Did you see that on the T.V. about conspiracy it showed these laws up for what they are. Anyhow Rose, give my regards to Peter, Colin, Richard and Gerry and thank them for me. I just hope I can repay them for believing in my innocence. Well Rose, there is not much more to tell you. Give everyone at home my regards. I am surprised that I have not heard from Jeanie. She usually writes regularly but she hasn't wrote for a couple months. Anyhow Rose, as I said not much more to say. Give Dawn and Ricky all my love and kisses and tell them I think of them all the time. I send you all my love. I miss you with all my heart. You are never out my thoughts and I pray that I will be home again with you and the children soon. I love you with all my heart. Write soon. XXXXXXXX Love You. X George.

make?" I really didn't know what impact it would have. The next morning there were reporters everywhere, I couldn't believe it.

And then they had to appear in court, all for digging a bit of dirt up. I was really shocked. But what they did will never die.

5

OPENING UP
THE GATES

We had to go all the way to Leeds for the trial. We only had one coach, but if you'd have seen the squad cars you would have thought we'd had a hundred. I shouted, "The others are on their way!"

When we got into court, this copper got up and gave his evidence, and my Colin jumped the dock. "You Judas!" Whatever he said, Colin said it wasn't the truth.

We all had a sit-down in the road outside the Leeds court. About seven of them got arrested. My poor sister, God rest her soul, was petrified. They had to take her to hospital, she fainted when they put her in the police van. She'd never been in a police station, never mind in the nick.

When Peter was imprisoned I came running out of court, screaming, "A man can molest a kid and get probation, and yet for digging a bit of dirt up he gets eighteen months!" Okay, Peter had 'a suspended on top of a suspended', but where's the justice in it?

Colin went to prison too, and he'd never been in a nick in his life. He got six months.

Colin used to ask me however did I keep coming

backwards and forwards to visit; he said it would have done his head in. He was a big fellah, my brother, but I saw him change. He was a bit like me, I suppose, sprightly. But then he left a wife and three kids struggling.

PETER

That very first night after I'd turned myself in, we'd all ended up in Yorkshire at what they called the Bridewell – another name for the prison cells or the police station. It was in the centre of Leeds, and I remember it was like a fucking carnival down there. All the prisoners were singing rebel songs, we were causing chaos. Once they had incarcerated us, we had to appear every Monday to get an extension from the magistrate so they could keep us inside.

I did have to recognise that I'd done so much of this stuff that they could make a case for keeping me in, because I was a proven recidivist. I was like a bouncing ball, I was always going to come back at them. But that shouldn't have applied to the others. Every time that we appeared at the magistrate's court each Monday morning, the building was ringed by police. They took each of us in our own individual police van, handcuffed between two police officers. The whole thing was over the top, and all of this was working in our favour. I mean, what were we going to do, for God's sake?

The others were all brave, especially Colin and this young American girl, Geri. She was originally in fucking Risley remand centre in Lancashire, and it was a hellhole. So many women have topped themselves there, it's still a terrible place to put a woman today. She was really courageous. She got bail at one point but wouldn't take it, refused to go home until we came home. In the end we fucking made her. She was a feminist and she was hard to handle, we even had a row on the way up. She had her own mind, but she was dedicated to us. She fought for the campaign and she was principled.

It's a great sadness in my life that she died and I never knew anything about it. I would like to have been there, I'd like to have spoken to her. She died at the age of about forty, over ten years ago now.

When I think of all the things I'd done, my sentence of eighteen months wasn't a bad cop. People had told me I might be getting three years. If I'd have behaved myself I'd have been out in under ten months. But I didn't behave myself.

My Shirley is a strong girl and she was behind me right from the beginning. She got on with it. I had mates who came round to make sure there was always food on the table; one mate used to come round every Saturday evening to make sure the kids had sweets and drinks.

There were parcels coming up, money was being put through the letterbox, food parcels, but no names, nothing. The Who did a benefit for us at the Charlton football ground. They had George Davis T-shirts. Rose and Shirley went on stage with the band.

Armley prison is like a witch's castle. It's awful. It's old and dingy, you can imagine witches flying all around it, it is the most frightening, horrible place.

We used to do that twice a week, Shirley Chappell and me. It took some doing, all those miles up to Leeds.

We had a sit-down in there because they wouldn't let them have their washing. I said, "But it's not a luxury, it's a necessity, they've got to have a change of washing!"

ROSE DEAN-DAVIS

In replying to this letter, please write on the envelope:—

Number W/997095 Name HUGHES E.

H.M. REMAND CENTRE, RISLEY,
WARRINGTON ROAD,
RISLEY,
WARRINGTON, CHESHIRE

21/10 qu

30·10·75

Dear Rosie,

Thanks for your letter & postal order. I feel quite wealthy now if only I get a chance to spend it sometime.

How are things coming for George? Has the registrar of the criminal appeals court replied yet?

Could you send me (if we don't come out this week) Richard & Chris's and Jean's addresses? (Is that how Jean spells her name, or is it Jeanne or what?)

I hope Deana is staying well. Tell little Rick I'm getting ever so toughened up in here, and when I get out he'd just better watch out!

I've just wrote a letter saying that there was going to be a bit in the Mirror on the

wives angle. Did it come off & was it well done? Not before time either.

What happened as a result of the talk with the M.P.? I assume you mean Mikardo. He's sometimes very helpful. Here I suppose all he can do is ask a question in the house. That M.P. Price got those three boys off after persistant effort.

There's nothing in the way of news to tell you. I don't do all that much (except sometimes the wrong thing).

Please don't worry about not visiting. You have your hands full coming up to see Colin and going down to see George.

Give my love to the kids and the rest of your family. Thanks again for the money.

Eric

PS Speaking of money, did you remember a contribution to "Jan" at Eastbourne House? I think we did mean things to their phone bill.

114

They moved us out between the visiting hall and the gate. I said, "Come on Shirl, sit down here!"

"I'll call the police!"

"You can call the British Army if you want to, we ain't moving!" So they sent the deputy governor down. They could have avoided all that. He just said, "Give me their washing," and he took it.

How many wives would have put up with what Peter's wife did? I probably would have, but then a lot of women would not. They'd have said, "Look, you've got a wife and family!" But that girl took it.

Shirley really is a lovely girl and a good mum. She's got three sons and a daughter: Little Peter, Tylene, Daniel and Michael. Daniel was only weeks old when we took him up to Leeds and sat on the floor in the courtyard. Only a babe in arms.

When Peter was in prison I walked into Scotland Yard and asked to see the Commissioner of Police. The girl behind the desk laughed. "It's like asking to see the Queen!" I said, "Well, he's a public servant, and I'm not leaving here till I've seen someone!" They sent someone down to me – he was quite senior, a chief inspector, someone high up. But I think the Commissioner must have been in bed, it was about eleven o'clock at night.

I went back to the Law Courts with Ian Cameron and Martin Walker, the guys who did all the design for the campaign. I did myself up in glasses and a hat, as I was recognisable by this time and there were always reporters or someone else outside. So I sort of slipped by.

When we walked in court, they looked up as if to say, "Why are these people interested?" It was a property case, we must have looked odd. We all sat in different rows.

"When I bang my foot, you get up and scream," Martin told me. And did I scream!

"It's a year ago today that you sentenced an innocent man!"

It was the same judge who'd sentenced George, Sebag Shaw – I always called him Shitbag Shaw. And he completely ignored me. "Oh, it's her again," was his attitude – though the clerk of the court said, "Out, out!" It was the highest court in the land and I should have got six months.

But people like Martin and Ian, who were very well-educated, stuck up for their principles. They knew injustice when they saw it, they were idealists, and that's why they got in touch with us.

I went to court in Chiswick, because someone told me that Charlie Lowe, the grass, was about to be questioned about something and I was told that George's name was going to be mentioned. Each person that went in the court was searched and asked why they were there. "I'm a trainee journalist," I said, as I had a load of papers in my hand. When George wasn't mentioned I got up and screamed out in court: "It's men like you who are putting innocent men away!" Of course, they just threw me out of the court. They realised who I was then as all the reporters were outside I was taken for a nutter, but I knew what I was doing. There was a policeman quite high up in the force who was done for taking bungs, he did time for it. I threw flour over him outside the court.

I bought two flares and sat at the top of the Monument with Martin and Bev, Geri the American girl's friend. There were three of us, chained together and masked, throwing all the leaflets from the top. I paid £25 each for the flares, that was a lot of money then, you can imagine the smoke and all the fire engines. It was like a wakeup call for London. When

Top left: I don't know how old my dad was here, but it looks like he'd only just joined the army – my mum said he falsified his age. My dad and his brothers were all great big men.

Top right: It's funny to think of a kid getting married at sixteen now. I never realised how young we looked – more in George's case than mine.

Bottom: My mum is to the right of me, with my sister's youngest and a neighbour's boy. My mother-in-law is on the left and my brothers Colin and David, the youngest, to the right.

Top: I was a 'beefeater' in the Tower Tavern restaurant at the Tower of London. That's Jeannie Ishmail next to me – I got her the job, I don't think she'd worked before.

Bottom left: We went to Spain for a long weekend, in March 1974, but it was cold. Rick was only eight then. It was two months before George was nicked for the LEB job.

Bottom right: This is from Linda Calvey's twenty-first birthday party, in 1969. Linda never had a hair out of place and she was a very pretty girl. It's so sad how her life turned out

Top: We're all done up for a special banquet at Plantation House, that's me on the left. This was in the late sixties, prior to all the trouble.

Bottom: This is Spain in '74. There's Derek Felstead on the right, next to George, and Mickey Ishmail, third from left. It was freezing, I don't know how Derek could wear shorts!

Top: This is Peter Chappell [*left*] at Bethnal Green. Colin [*right*] has his back to the camera while my other brother Jimmy [*far right*] is lying down. The protest blocked the roads.

Bottom: The 'Justice for George Davis' placard was designed by Martin Walker. Aunt Jo is on the left at this march, underneath the umbrella.

George's leave to appeal has been turned down, the Court having refused to listen to fresh evidence. But the fight is not over –in fact it's just beginning! We will be picketing New Scotland Yard right through Christmas Eve, Christmas Day, and Boxing Day. Please join us if you can for any part of that time.

Our thanks to everyone who has helped in the campaign. WE WISH YOU ALL A VERY HAPPY CHRISTMAS AND NEW YEAR. Let's make next Christmas an even happier one, and 1976 a year for justice and freedom!

Dina, Ricky, and Rose Davis,
59, Belton Way,
Bromley-by-Bow,
London, E.3.

rd (Report)

op: There's Aunt Jo right up the front (she had some guts), little Rick with Deana down the back, and my Jimmy's boy with the checked shirt in the middle.

entre left: This is my mother- and father-in-law, Ann and George, with Mickey Ishmail's mum behind them. Ann was a big woman, but look at that little placard she's carrying!

ottom inset: When George went for his appeal against conviction and it was turned down, he had these cards printed and we used to hand them out everywhere.

ottom right: The second march, the 4th May 1975, to Downing Street. Look at the amount of police there! Peter used to row with the copper at the front, who was from the City Police.

Top: George didn't know Violet and Charlie Kray [*left*], but they'd been to see the twins in Parkhurst and got the same boat over. The only connection was that I'd worked with Violet.

Below: George had just got in the car before me. What a gentleman! On the left of the copper in the middle you can see Colin [moustache] and to the right Mickey [tinted glasses].

Bottom inset: I think I was in a daze. This was at Waterloo, within five minutes of George leaving the train. He was right at the back so we had to walk the length of the platform.

op: George is looking up toward our flat, where everyone was out on the landing.
here's Colin, laughing, behind George, Mickey to the right and Patsy Clarke, smiling,
ehind Mickey.

ottom left: Peter Hain is advertising his own book here, with George holding a copy.
must have been at one of the few debates George attended soon after he got out.

ottom right: If that isn't taking the pee! ... When George got out of prison, him, me and
olin actually went to the cricket at Headingley.

Top: This is (*right to left*) me, Karen Ishmail and Deana at my nephew's wedding, nearly thirty years ago. Karen was Deana's friend and she still keeps in touch.

Below: This is my Deana in her dining room. She was a good cook, and she loved entertaining. She was a lovely girl.

Bottom inset: Me and George at a family wedding about fifteen years ago, doing our best not to look at each other.

the fireman got up he went, "Fucking 'ell! Now I've got to go and get the cutters!"

There was a picture that won a prize, of a girl carrying a 'George Davis Is Innocent' placard. She was six months pregnant and it made it look like he was the one that did it.

You had to have a sense of humour during the campaign, or you'd have sunk.

PETER

The campaign was a group of people defending themselves and trying to get those in power – the state, the judiciary – to think again and have a look at this case. To start with, I didn't see things like that. My class perspective only came about after Headingley, during my confinement, due to the stuff that I was reading. Then I took an actual class-conscious position. Before that, I was aware that I was working class but I acted more unconsciously.

I know now that everything you do is bloody political. All the decisions that rule our lives are political decisions. But Rosie was a working girl, waiting tables.

The J.A.I.L. movement[1] was mainly set up while I was in prison, just after I dug the pitch up and I was remanded to Armley jail. It involved Peter Hain, who dedicated a couple of books to me that he'd written, including one about the police. Hain wasn't an MP at the time but he was a radical, he was in the Liberal Party and he led the anti-Apartheid campaign in this country. He used to lead big demonstrations at the rugby grounds and things like that. Then he was fitted

---

1 *J.A.I.L. was an acronym of Justice Against The Identification Laws. It was set up in the mid-1970s as a direct outgrowth of the campaigns to free George Davis and other prisoners convicted solely on identification evidence.*

up on a charge. That's how he came into contact with us – it was the same thing as George, ID evidence. There were many people who thought at the time that it was something to do with the South African police boss.

I have to say that, although I wasn't political at the time, the campaign did come out of an intense period from 1968 onwards. There were student riots in Paris and at the American Embassy. Nearer the time, in '72, the Heath government had put the country on a three-day week and jailed five dockers. All the dockers had mobilised and gone to Pentonville jail. They weren't going away until the guys were released, which is exactly what happened.

So there were big political struggles going on at the time. All these things were influencing me. I wasn't active but I was there in the audience, looking at it all and taking it in.

The campaign, what it meant and the people involved in it, were precious to me. While I was in prison I made a decision to change my life. I had to be true to all those people, and to all the things that I'd learned during that campaign. And the world opened up to me. All sorts of influences ran through me. I'm not like these young middleclass lads and lasses that get involved in politics in their younger years and then give it all up, I've stuck with it. And it all stemmed from knowing that George Davis wasn't there that morning. I've learned all sorts of things and I can't go backwards. I've got strong principles and I won't give them up.

GEORGE

I think Peter became a little bit political, but Rose and I were certainly not. I'm not even sure we ever voted. We weren't anarchists in any shape or form, we weren't upset about the government. We were upset about the police.

THE WARS OF ROSIE

In replying to this letter, please write on the envelope:—

Number 1890   Name DAVIES

H.M. PRON.
ALBANY,
NEWPORT,
ISLE OF WIGHT

Dear Rose,
    I hope you got that message alright from the welfare man. They will be company for you. I saw Rich got bail. Give him my regards. I wrote to Peter Shore and told him the police were victimising all my friends and that it is discusting Peter and colin not getting bail. I got Deana's letter and she said she had to go back into hospital on Monday. She did not say why. Whats wrong with her? You never said anything in your letter. Rose write and tell me or phone the welfare if anything is wrong. You know how I worry. Well Rose, I still haven't heard from the appeal court. I was talking to a fellow who was weighed off the same day as me. There was eight of them and they have all appealed. He has already had leave to XX Dad he was going up nex XXXX it was

put back until December. Yet I haven't even been given leave to appeal. It seems like they are digging me out. Its obvious that my appeal went in the same time as theirs. Can you get Wendy Mantle to push them a bit. Also Rose, tell her I sent to the appeal court telling them why I want to change solicitors. Rose, do you think you could get me a pair of moccasins? Only the shoes in here make my feet smell. Dont say it, I know I amapeest. I see that you had the march on Sunday. The paper said there were only about 100 people. Still, if there were only 10 at least its a show. Well Rose, I am going to sign off now. I will drop Deana and Ricky a couple of lines on the other page. Give everyone at home my thanks and also my regards. Tell Colin and Peter to keep their chins up. They will get bail eventually. I send you my heart. I love you more than any thing and I miss you so much it hurts. I pray I will be home with you again soon. I XXXX XXXXXX

Hello my angels, how are you both. I am well myself and looking forward to seeing you both again soon. Dea. I was choked about you being in hospital. I pray to God you are better now. You looked so lovely on my visit and you looked very well. Anyhow Dea, look after yourself and dont worry about your fat old dad, I will be alright. Well Boysie, how are you? I haven't heard from you since you sent me a birthday card, except when I saw you on the visit. I hear you are being a very good boy for your Mum. Well Boy I am proud of you and Deana. I love you both so much. I pray for you both everynight and that I will be home with yous again soon. I tell you kids, when I do come home, I will smother you both with kisses and please God we will go on a nice holiday. Anyhow kids, time to sign off now. I send you both all my love and kisses Always thinking of you both XXXX
love
    Daddy. XXXX

When Peter and Colin were away up in Leeds, Gerry Healy got in touch, the really militant leader of the Workers Revolutionary Party.[2] We got a phone call one day, me and Shirley, to say that he would like to see us. He sent this beautiful great big black Daimler round to take us over to south London.

It was really cloak-and-dagger. Me and her kept looking at one another. We went into this builder's yard, pulled up in the car, got out and went into this factory. We were taken into this room where he was sitting at the desk.

"Sit down, ladies. This room is padded, no one can hear us." It was scary.

He banged his fist on the desk. "What you ladies have done is wonderful! I want you to get your husbands to join . . ."

We went, "Oh yeah, we will." When we got out of there, I said, "Fucking lunatic!" We weren't going for any of that.

And yet politics is very interesting, when you start looking into things. You lead your life, you go to work, you come home, you're in your own little world. When these sorts of things happen, it broadens your horizons.

I got a phone call about the campaign: "Is it political?" I said, "It's got nothing to do with politics!" He must have thought, "You stupid woman." I didn't even look at it that way, but it became very political in the end.

And I never dreamt in a million years that I would ever get involved with people like Peter Hain. He jumped on our bandwagon after he got accused of robbing a building society in Putney. He was one of the Young Liberals then, but of course he's part of the Labour government now.

---

2 *Post-imprisonment, subsequent to his personal politicisation, Peter Chappell would join the WRP.*

He got in touch with Peter, I think. He was waiting to go to court and I suppose he thought he'd find out how we got our campaign going. He obviously didn't do the robbery. His family came out of South Africa and they had to flee. When you heard some of the stories that his parents told us around the dinner table, about how they visited friends the day before they were executed, it made you think, does this really go on in the world? But obviously it did. What a terrible way to live.

His mum and dad were *lovely* people, they made us very welcome. His dad kept saying to me, "Don't call me Mr Hain, call me Walter." After a glass of wine – I wasn't a drinker – it was, "Good night Wally!" ('Walter' is 'Wally' in the East End.)

After that I did become very interested in politics, in what was happening in the community. When I hear people say, "I don't vote, it's a waste of time," I get angry. They're always the first to complain, but if you don't put yourself out then no one's going to put themselves out for you, are they?

People were coming to us then. Dolly, Charlie Kray's wife, was fighting for George Ince. She got him off of a murder charge because she was in bed with him at the time.[3] But she

---

3 *Charlie Kray was still serving a ten-year sentence for his disputed role as accessory to Jack McVitie's murder when his wife's indiscretion became known. Her lover, Ince, was tried twice at Chelmsford Crown Court for the November 1972 murder of Muriel Patience and the shootings of her husband and daughter at the Barn restaurant in Braintree, Essex. In the second instance, it was the apprehension of John Brook with the murder weapon that got Ince acquitted in May 1973, rather than Dolly's candour alone. When the Free George Davis Campaign began in 1974, its echoes of the lower-profile Free George Ince Campaign (also supported by Up Against The Law), together with the similarity of the names, initially misled some people into confusing the two. By the time of Dolly Kray's brief association with Rose and the Davis campaign, she was seeking guidance to overturn Ince's subsequent fifteen-year sentence for armed robbery. This time, though, all the evidence was against him.*

used us and then didn't want to know us later. She thought her shit didn't stink, always worried about her appearance. Me, if you look at some of the photos I'm in, I couldn't have cared less what I looked like.

I never knew when there were going to be press there. I wasn't putting any makeup on, I couldn't give a shit really. I didn't like being recognised. I'd sit on a train, and I could see people whispering, "That's George Davis's wife." But then that's the price you pay. I get angry when I hear these pop stars whining, "The press are always at me!" The press have made them, haven't they?

RICK

Me and Deana used to have a laugh at some of the people in the campaign – 'soap dodgers', as we'd call them. There were some stinkers. Deana used to bleach the cups out because some of them were so rough, all these longhaired smokers. When you walked in the house afterwards it just stank. They were there to help us, so you can't slag them off. Quite a few of them were anti-establishment, which I suppose is what we wanted. Obviously the more the merrier. Some of them were very intelligent people, but just didn't like washing. But there were some nutters, even down to the reporters.

When we wanted someone to stand bail at Leeds, it was a hundred grand or something ridiculous. In those days we never knew anyone with that sort of money. This man rang up calling himself Lord Amery, and said he was willing to put up the bail money.

"Ooh Shirley, a lord!" Shirley and her mum scrubbed that place spotless. Then the knock comes at the door, it's this scruffy looking bloke with long greasy hair and a tattered velvet jacket on. In he comes. Her mum said, "If he's a lord, I'm a fucking lady!" He had unwashed hair all the way down his back, a typical bohemian type. "I'll come to Leeds and stand bail," he said. We were over the moon. "What time are you meeting the coach?"

It was four o'clock outside Mile End station. He turned up, true to his word, with a straw bucket bag that had a load of papers sticking out. They stopped at a service station on the way down, and I was sitting there talking to Pat Cross of the *Advertiser*. One of my sisters went to me, "Oi! See 'im, Lord Amery? I've caught him going down the bins, eating bits of bread!" My other sister said, "He nicked a packet of sweets off the service counter."

If he was a lord you might think he'd look the part, but he had dirty washing in his bag and he took out a pair of knickers to blow his nose. I thought, "Oh no, this is going to be a waste of time." We got to the court, the usher checked him out and, sure enough, he didn't have a penny.

But how could you be horrible to him? He meant well, but he was nutty.

We got on the coach coming back. Halfway along the M1, Mickey Ishmail said to the driver, "Stop 'ere, mate!" We stopped, and he chucked dear Lord Amery off. As he got his bag, all his dirty washing came flying out.

I felt terrible. I said, "You shouldn't have done that, Mick."

"Fucking nutter!" he said.

It wasn't only him, we met quite a few. One woman had 'George Davis Is Innocent' written all the way up the side of her legs.

One night someone rang me up: "Can you get a solicitor? I know things . . . I can get George out."

So what do you do? You're clutching at straws. We took him along to a pub owned by Jimmy Sheehan, who was a solicitor. I said, "Jim, this man's got something. I don't know him but he won't talk to me, he'll only talk to a solicitor."

"Right, young man, what have you got to say?"

"Nothing . . ." he said, "I don't know nothing . . ."

Another nutter. They just wanted a bit of attention, I think.

PETER

The essence of that campaign, one of the things that made it so successful, was the ability to penetrate the middleclass professionals, people with talents; people like the actors at the Half Moon Theatre, who put on a play for us; people like Martin Walker, who had a real skill in designing posters. Many good solicitors today were radicals who quite famously cut their teeth on our campaign, like Gareth Peirce, the Welsh girl who does all these big trials now. Michael Mansfield QC defended me at Liverpool and got me bail after the Headingley trial. Lord Gifford defended me. We leafleted all the Inns of Court, in the Temple and Lincoln's Inn Fields. All the solicitors knew about that campaign. We put slogans up on the walls of their buildings down there. It penetrated layers that people like us weren't able to penetrate before. It made us all sorts of friends in high places.

The play, George Davis Is Innocent OK, *was put on because I was constantly searching through the news, making contacts. I didn't go to bed, I'd be working till late at night, phoning people and writing. It really was constant. I took myself up to Aldgate, to Alie Street where the theatre was, and watched a play for the first time since I'd left school. It was about two air raid wardens in the war and it* just blew me away. The Half Moon was just a flea pit, wooden floorboards and benches to sit on, but it was a proper theatre.

In fact Martin Walker designed the poster for that particular play. I spoke to some of the actors and told them about the George Davis campaign. Shortly after that I dug the pitch up. It was while I was in prison that they decided to get it together and actually put it on.

In replying to this letter, please write on the envelope:—

Number 1890   Name DAVIS

H.M. PRISON,
ALBANY,
NEWPORT,
ISLE OF WIGHT.

Dear Rose,

I was really pleased to see you today. I can't tell you how much it means to me to see you. You looked lovely today, but then you always look lovely to me. Well Rose, as we were saying today, it looks like I will be away again for christmas. I wonder if those slags from the robbery squad will think of me in here. I hope they choke on their turkey bones. Mind you Rose they are so low and snakey. They only think of fitting other poor bastards up. When you tell me that Matthews looks ill, I feel elated. It could not happen to a more deserving person. I call him a person but it is not what I would call him if this letter was not censored. Rose, I have nightmares about him and everytime he winds [...] in his yacht. I hope [...]

No. 265   30143   8-2-68

Rose, how about those 3 boys being cleared of that murder. They were supposed to have confessed and yet they could not have done it. No one is going to confess to something they never done. One paper said that the copper who nicked them should resign. It never said nothing about nicking the dirty no good slag. Rose, you would never believe what they do, would you? One fellow who was in here and was pardoned, had supposed to have confessed to a robbery when he was pardoned, the police said that he was drunk when he confessed, so therefore the police were not at fault. I wouldn't mind, but they get away with it. Rose, I have just read a book about Hanratty. I thought my case was bad enough, but you should read this. Its called "Who Killed Hanratty." They fitted him up so blatantly, it is unbelievable. Then they hung him. Rose, since this has happened to me, I have lost all my faith in British Justice. As far as I'm concerned, there is no such thing. All you seem to see in the papers is that

someone has been wrongly imprisoned.
You get people screaming about it
in the papers, but they wont get off
their arses to stop it. If these people
were like my friends, then someone
would have to do something about
these injustices. Thats the trouble with
this country. Too many big mouths and
not enough with guts who will stand
up and be counted. Well Rose, thats got
that off my chest. I was pleased to
hear that Peter, Colin and Gerry are
all in good spirit. Rose, give them all
my fondest regards and tell them they
are never out of my thoughts. Give
everyone my regards and tell my mom
I will be writing tomorrow. Tell Aunt
Joe I will drop her a line also Big
Jean. (Micks mom). Anyhow Rose, just to
remind you, will you ask Wendy Mantle
about a set of transcripts. I would
like to know what is in them
and will you ask how to come to
see me as soon as possible. Rose,
tell her to push it and try to
get my appeal up as soon as she
possibly can. Tell her I dont like it
in here and I want to

Seriously though Rose, I dont see why
they can't hear it this year. By christmas
it will be nearly Ten months since I
was weighed off. Anyhow Rose, I am going
to say goodbye once again. Give Deana and
Ricky all my love and kisses and tell
them I think of them all the time.
I send you all my love and kisses. I
love you with all my heart. I long for
the day I am with you again. You are
in my thoughts 24 hours a day. You are
my life. I Love You.
                    George.

I LOVE
YOU
XXXXXXXXX XX XXXXX XXXX
P.S. Dont forget the magazine.
I Love You. I love you. I love and miss
I Love You. I love you. XX you. XXXX
I Love You. I love you. XXXXXXXX

ROSE DEAN-DAVIS

When I got out of prison on bail, one of the draconian conditions I was released under was that I mustn't have anything to do with the campaign. But I went to the afternoon theatre, saw the play and it just blew my brains out. As I went into the theatre, they had quoted from one of my letters that I wrote to Shirley and it was above the stage. Now, to see my own words up there above the stage was enormously impressive. It all just seemed so profound, though it wasn't really. The play was written by a chap called Shane Connaughton, an Irish playwright.

The play was by a leftwing playwright. I think Peter got in touch with them about it. Barristers and solicitors went to see it. Police officers went to see it. It was only supposed to be on for a month, but it went on for a lot longer. It was at the Half Moon Theatre, which was in Aldgate at that time. It was a tiny little theatre, but it was too political to put it on in the West End at that time. They had hardly any props but it was brilliant.

Every night they had a collection and that money went into the fund. They raised quite a lot of money. It was used for coaches, rather than fines. People filled that theatre every night.

I went and saw it about six times. I couldn't get over it. It was our life story up to the arrest. They had a bit of humour in it, and they had Alan Ford who's since been in Guy Ritchie's films. He played Mickey Ishmail. I've got photos of all of us together at Peter's, about ten years ago. It was sad really, because we all lost touch with one another. They all got on with their lives and I had to get on with mine.

If you could do it now though it probably wouldn't have

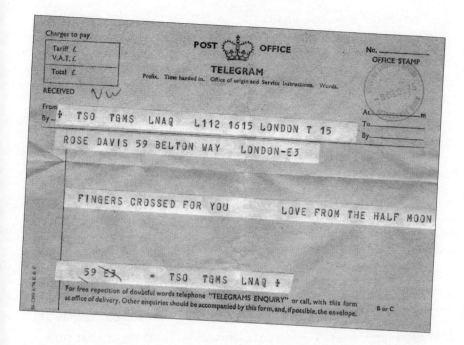

the same effect, as people had to know what the campaign was about.

PETER

There was only one point during the prison sentence when I was at a low. I was in the hospital wing having a minor operation to my nose. I'd been having fluid through my nose, so they took some bone away. I'd been incarcerated then for about three months. It was the spring of '76. I was at a stage where I was beginning to think, "What will I do if I'm released and he's still inside?" That was beginning to dawn on me.

But it was only that one day after the operation that I felt low. Once I was over it, I was making plans. I was going to sink the fucking HMS Belfast, that idea was beginning to germinate. We'd have done it very simply, just by opening the

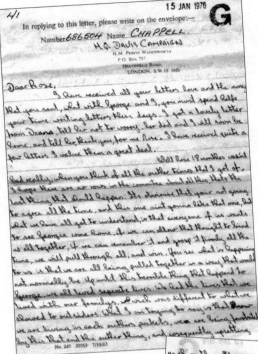

41

15 JAN 1976

G

In replying to this letter, please write on the envelope:—

Number 686504 Name CHAPPELL

H.Q. DAVIS CAMPAIGN

H.M. PRISON WANDSWORTH

P.O. BOX 757

HEATHFIELD ROAD,

LONDON, S.W.18 3HS

Dear Rose,

I have received all your letters love and the ones that you sent, what with George and I, you must spend all your time writing letters these days. I got a lovely letter from Jeans, tell her not to worry, her dad and I will soon be home, and tell her thank you for me Rose. I have received quite a few letters I value them a great deal.

Well Rose 18 months wasn't bad really, when you think of all the outher times that I got it, I hope there are no more in the countries but all this that's the last thing that shall happen. Its obvious that your not going to agree all the time, and this one aint gonna like that one, but what we have all got to understand, is that everyone of us wants to see George come home, if we can allow that thought to bind us all together, if we can remember it and grasp it firmly all the time, we will pull through all, and win. You see what is happening to us is that we are all being pulled together in a way that would not normally be. Up until this terrible thing that happend to George, we all lived separate lives. We had the lives that we lived with our families, which was different to what we showed to outsiders. What I am trying to say is that now we are living in each other pockets, we are being forced by this that and the other thing, and consequently upsetting

No. 243 30563 7/10/63

each outher. If we can only see this and recognize it for what it is, we will be O.K. What you should do here, is to say this at the next meeting, you see it is easier to see when you are on the outside looking in, as I am at the moment, its not so easy when your in the middle of it all, and I know how bloody akward and difficult I am myself. Any way think about it, and see what you think.

I heard Shirley on the Radio the outher day I was really pround of her, and it definitly makes the BIG job a lot easier. Shirly sent the East London to me but I havent received it, tell her not to worry but the next time she wants me to have a paper tell her to send it through TOS the newsagent, and make sure he stamps it with the shops name or let Cross might be able to do it and make through the Advertizer, but I must be stamped with a name. Rose tell Shirley that whenever the news media get on to her about anything that has happend, such as a demo, tell her never to deny or admit anything. You see we should play this like Poker, let the media think what they like, and if the Fuzz come round Rose, refuse to speak to them, remember they are a lot trickier than us. Anouther thing that could be done is to let the media know that every sporting occasion, in fact every occasion where people are enjoying themselves, will be a legitimate target for the Davis Campaigners, and the committee should not send letters to the media outlining their type of policey, because of the coulacks, but there is more than one way to do this and I'm sure the committee could soon find one. Any way its only a suggestion. By the way dont answer any of these suggestions when you write back to me. ...

Rose I wonder if you could ask Paul Brighton how the shop is going only I am a little bit worried about the stockists and one or two other things, I will love to see the Governor when I get to Walton, to try and work something out.

That sounds like very good news (Record Co.) especially as they put it in writing I would very much like to see something come of that. Could you tell Martin & Ian that I spoke to a clerk at the Sandwich of David Whitehouse before I got sent down, I asked him if David Whitehouse could help Martin & Ian with the book, and he gave me the impression that he would be willing, anyway Rich has got his number in the book, the best time to get him is about 4.30 or 5 p.m. The committee can Advertise the march on the three local radio stations, all they have to do is phone in on the PHONE in' shows, we really do need a lot of advertising for this march, I am sure we have a lot of support its a question of mobilising it.

Well Rose how are you yourself, I hope your not letting any of this get you down remember when your on the floor the only way is up, we've got all the good times to come by the time I come home I don't suppose I will be able to communicate with you lot, what with me O levels in English Language & Sociology, and you'll still say ello and all that, but I won't be able to mix wiv yer cos us students are funny like that. Course I won't be able to take any body home to over dinner from the University, not in the way Shirley and em kids talk, but for informing

for me. Hey anyway keep smiling, and try and be a bit more tougher with these reporters, you haven't got to be nasty to them, just tell them where its at.

By the way here, a lot of people have been writing to me could you tell them that I really appreciate a letter, and I am very grateful to all of them I read them all two or three times and more. By the time you get this letter Rose I should be in Walton. I hope so anyway.

Still love I don't know when I will be able to write to you again so look after yourself, and tell the committee that I am with them all the way, and I understand these pollins. If I can lend any support they've just to say the word. Give them all my best brothers I only wish I had words to tell them how grateful I am to all of them, I love you all Rose, and tell my Shirley I love her and my kids more than anything I know were all fighting it Rosé but it won't always be like this, and were gonna win, and how. See you soon Rose, stay and get up with Shirley and Martin on the next visit.

All my love and best wishes   Eric   X †.

P.S. tell that dirty little fucker Ricky to weed behind his ears give my love to Deano, tell Jo keep writing

P.P.S. and tell Shirley Chappell she is a very lucky girl to have a body love her like I do. XXXXXXXXXXX
(really Mr Carrot.)   xxx Eric & Shirley XXXXXXXXX
                                       & Peter and David

stopcocks on the front of the ship. The thing would have sunk very quickly. But it took a little bit more organising, because we'd have had to go aboard the ship, reconnoitre it and get down into the bowels to seal it off so we could do our work.

As soon as I came out of the hospital, I started printing 'George Davis Is Innocent' on prison-issue shirts. I was back in the fire again. No sooner had I done that, I was up before the beak and sentenced to loss of three months' remission.

And while I was down there, serving out the punishment, he was released. All those doubts that were beginning to creep in suddenly dissipated.

GEORGE

I knew what was happening on the outside, but I didn't realise to what extent. Rose used to send me letters and they gave you your mail on a Tuesday lunchtime.

Tuesday lunchtime. No fucking letters. I was on a horticultural course, I only did it so I could be out in the open. (I didn't really know anything about plants – I mean, fucking hell, japonica?) Anyhow, we wound up. All of a sudden a screw came in.

"Davis, the AG (Acting Governor) wants to see you!"

Now I'm thinking the worst. I haven't got a letter from Rose and now I've got a call-up to the AG. Something's happened. Got into the wing, we had a screw there called Hudson, or Lofty as we used to call him. He wanted to find out what the matter was.

"Wait in here, young 'un," he told me.

"No, I'm alright, Lofty." I was just standing there.

The AG came in with another PO (principal officer). "Follow me, Davis." We went up into his office.

"I have a letter here from the Home Secretary. It says here that, owing to the weakness of the evidence against you, we've got to release you today. But you haven't got a pardon."[4]

"What did you say? I can go home?"

"Yes. But understand that you haven't got a pardon."

"I can go?"

"Yes!"

"That'll do me."

The day he was released, his aunt and me were in my sitting room. Not that I'm fat now, but I was like a rake by then. It came over the radio that the Home Secretary had released him. We were screaming!

Oh, they should have fucking kept him there . . .

---

4 On 11th May 1976, the Queen complied with a request from the Home Secretary, Roy Jenkins, that she exercise the little-used Royal Prerogative of Mercy in the case of George Davis. After nearly two years of campaigning, it came as a sudden bolt from the blue to his family, friends and supporters.

6

HERO'S WELCOME

George was released on the eleventh of May, just before my birthday. I'd heard little snippets from the papers. Different reporters had been ringing me up, asking, "Have you heard anything?" Then I heard on the radio that he'd been released. You knew then that it was gospel. I've got a photo of Aunt Jo and me screaming in my front room. I was shocked.

GEORGE

I didn't think it was going to happen how it did, as quickly as it did. But there was always something in my mind that told me I was never going to do that sentence. I suppose that's hope. But it was always in my mind.

By this time, when they let me out, the sentence was down to seventeen years. They took off the three for wounding with intent, and the rest was made concurrent rather than consecutive, so the sentences ran together.

As lawyers I had John Marriage, who's since died, and David Whitehouse, who were both brilliant. They just believed in me totally. They had a job to do and they

*defended loads of people, but they believed in me, as David
still does now.*

The next thing was that the papers came. I don't know if
it was *The Mirror* or *The Mail*, but they took me to
Waterloo to meet him. Shirley was with me, and the
reporter was saying, "We've not seen anything like this
since VE Day."

I went, "Hark at him, not seen nothing like this since VD
Day." Shirley pissed herself laughing, I hadn't realised what
I'd said.

It was packed, and not just with people coming home
from work. Who else should be there but Charlie and old
Violet Kray? They came back on the same train as George,
with all the reporters. I worked with her, she was one lovely
lady – not at all flash, unlike the Krays' dad. (I only ever met
him once, and didn't like him.) I was waitressing, she was
washing up in the kitchen.

She was a sad mother, yet she always had a smile.
(Charlie's boy, Gary, who I believe was gay, loved his nan.
He used to take her abroad every year. He's dead now too,
it's all very sad.)

GEORGE
*I went outside and told my mate Alan (who's also dead
now), "They're letting me go."*

"Don't be silly."

*"They're fucking letting me go, son!" I let him take any
of my things that I didn't want.*

"Fuck me . . . you can get your leg over tonight!"

*By this time they've got to give me clothes out of the
reception, because I've got no clothes there and they want to*

get me out of the nick. By now there's a line of guys: "Good luck, George!" It's got round the nick that quickly.

They put me in one of those small minibus things, with a screw to take me to the harbour to get a ferry across. He briefed me up, told me what to do, he was a really nice screw. But even now I haven't realised how big it all is, even though I've seen bits and pieces.

I get on the ferry, and who gets on but Charlie Kray and Violet Kray. Rose apparently worked in a pub with Violet. Charlie had been out a while but the twins were still in Parkhurst, they'd been to visit them.

Charlie's looked over to me and I've nodded. He's nodded back and come over.

"Alright?"

"Yeah."

Of course he doesn't know who I am, but he knows the face from the local paper.

"They've just let me out."

"What?"

"They've just let me out! I'm George Davis!"

"Fuck me! Mother, it's Rose's George!"

I sat down to have a cup of tea. "Oh," old Violet said, "it's just like having one of my own home!" When we got to Portsmouth, Charlie said, there would be reporters waiting. I said, "No, why would they want to come all this way down?"

All of sudden they're there. I've done my nut. All I want to do is phone to see if Rose knows. I've tried to phone but of course our home number is engaged. Then the reporters tried to get me to have a drink. I said, "No, I'll have a coffee." Fucking hell, I hadn't had a drink in two years!

RAP

Radical Alternatives to Prison ‖ Eastbourne House, Bullard's Place, London, E.2. ‖ office hours: 01-981 0041
other times: 01-947 0489

May 12th, 1976

Dear George and Rose,

This is a brief note to say how happy I am for you both. You have
RAP's heartiest congratulations and well wishes.

If you are going to continue to campaign for a free pardon and for
Pete Chappell's release you are assurred of our continuing support. -
Keep us informed of what you're doing and we will carry-on publishing
your statements in the RAP newsletter.

All the very best. -

Yours for RAP,

Liz Middleton.

Liz Middleton

A Christian Action Project. Regd. Offices: 2, Amen Court, London, E.C.2.

RICK

*There was a kid in my class who lived round the corner to
me. I don't know how he knew. It was after lunchtime. He
came up and said to me, "Your dad's been released."
"What? No!" "Yeah, go down the office, they want to see
you." He came with me; the school secretary was sitting
there with the radio on. And then it came over the radio.*

*It must have been about three o'clock in the assembly
hall. We've gone into assembly and sat down at the back.
Then the headmistress said to me, "Richard Davis? We've
got some very good news for you" – this is in front of the
whole school, all the teachers were standing there – "your
father has been released."*

138

THE WARS OF ROSIE

Waaahh!!!

"Go on, you can go home!" I ran out of school, as it was only about ten minutes away. As I got home there were masses of people there. They were scaffolding our block and there were people on the roofs, it looked like thousands of them. It was just uproar. There were all the people on the estate, all the other people in the neighbourhood, all my mates were shouting at me. The cars, the mobs, everyone to do with the campaign, friends, family – it looked like there were a couple of thousand people there. I got in the shed and got all the banners out that we used to have for the marches.

Then I went with my nan down to the Today studios at Euston Road, where the old Capital Radio used to be, for an interview. We got taken into the green room, and who should be there but Batman – or Adam West, who used to play him. I used to love Batman, and I got Adam West's autograph.

I was just glad it was all over. Glad we could all get back to normal. No more visiting prisons, no more having to get on trains, no more going across on the Isle of Wight ferry in the freezing cold. But obviously, most of all, I wanted my dad back home.

Deana was already with my mum at home. As he came in the door we had the world's press there, as well as all the British photographers. They were fighting to get photos of him and as he came in the front room he just stood there.

When he went upstairs they took a picture of us – me, my mum, my sister and my dad – all standing there in my sister's bedroom. We all had to go upstairs because there were so many people. That was the photo that went on the front of all the papers.

I went back to school the next day, and all my mates were

going, "Oh look, there's you!" as were all the people in the shops. All the teachers were pleased too, they'd already known about what had happened. It'd just become part of our lives by then, we'd got used to it. You had to, didn't you? I suppose it's like living in a war zone, just a fact of life.

But I was kind of a little mini-celebrity in their midst.

PETER

George never wrote to me once in the entire time that I was inside. The day that he got released, I was at Walton jail in Liverpool. I'd been imprisoned on January the sixth 1976. He was released in the May of that year, so this is about four months after. I used to have my own little printing press at the time, which shows just how dedicated I was to the campaign. I worked in the tailoring shop, which is a very good job to have in the nick. Usually, if you get a job like that, you don't jeopardise it. But I made a stamp: 'George Davis Is Innocent OK'. There were about six of us on this big long table and it was our job to examine the regulation blue-striped shirts for the whole prison system, to make sure there weren't any cottons hanging.

So I'd made this stamp and got all the lads on the table involved in it. We'd be stamping these shirts on the shoulder, on the breast, I think we'd done about seventeen thousand – it might even have been more. The only way it came a-tumble was when they started to deliver the shirts throughout the system. Some prisoners were going around like it was a fucking medal on their shirt.

They couldn't prove that it was me because I was really careful, but they knew it was. So they brought me before the prison governor and a board of visitors. I lost three months of remission and got a month's solitary confinement. I did more than that in there, but that was just this particular time. Down in this prison dungeon you'd have a prison officer and also what was called a rep band, a trusted prisoner. He kept the punishment block spotlessly clean, and apart from when he came to the door with his radio I knew nothing at all. I wasn't seeing the papers or anything. We know how to isolate people in this country because we've been doing it for a long time.

What they used to do in solitary confinement was, at eight o'clock in the morning, your bed was taken out of the cell so all you had for the rest of the day, till eight o'clock that night, was a table, a chair, a pisspot in the corner and four walls. It was fucking freezing cold.

There's a bang on the door. "Peter, Peter, George Davis has been released!" He's got a radio and it's tuned into a broadcast from Waterloo station. George is just getting off the train and I can hear everyone cheering. I can hear George talking to a reporter. "Who do you thank for this, George?" And this fucking cunt, who I'm in solitary confinement for, says, "I've got to thank the Daily Mirror.*" The fucking* Daily Mirror! *And I'm in solitary confinement!*

I was fucking gutted. The Mirror *jumped on the bandwagon. They were the first people I went to, and they refused me because of* sub judice.

GEORGE
I had half a row with the Mirror, *because there had been a murder in Albany prison and they put me down as a prosecution witness. Their reporter came up and said, "Hello, I'm Alan Gale from the* Mirror.*"*

"Yeah, fuck off! You made me look like a fucking wrong 'un in the paper. I don't want to talk to you."

When the Mirror *came out the next day, Peter thought I'd said, "Thanks to the* Daily Mirror." *I didn't, but Peter had read it. He did not ever* hear *me say that. Whatever would I say thank you to the* Mirror *for? It was the* Mirror *doing their own verbal: "Thank God for Rose, thank God for the* Daily Mirror, *all I want to do is go home and have a bit of pie and mash."*

Then we came into Waterloo. The platform was full of people. I couldn't believe it. I thought, "Fucking hell, is this for me?" It was unbelievable.

You've come from a society where there's only a few people, then all of a sudden you've got thousands around you. You don't know what to do.

At first it was a shock to be home. I couldn't go anywhere, couldn't even go to the bloody toilet because someone would be following me. It wasn't frightening but it was uncomfortable.

That first night, we went out to the pub. One of our friends said, "My car's parked round the back, here's the keys. Go on, you and Rose go!"

So we went out the back of the pub, got in the car and went round to another pub near to where we lived, where there weren't so many people and my family were in there. We had a couple of drinks with them, then we went round to Shirley because Peter was still in Liverpool prison for digging up the pitch. And that was our day.

The next day, the kids got up and the bloody reporters were indoors. In the meantime, I couldn't find any of my shaving kit and I couldn't go in the toilet. I thought, "Fuck it!" I ran out and got in the car. Mickey Ishmail's mum, Jean, was around the corner. I just drove round there and parked the car up so I could use the bloody toilet.

Phoned Rose, told her, "I'm round Mick's mum's," so she knew where I was. All of a sudden she said, "Listen, I've got someone here, there's a girl who's gonna get us a press agent." So we wound up with a press agent handling us.

But I was still just me. I was the one who didn't like it. I was the one who stood back.

We went to the Tower Hotel, where either the Evening News *or the* Evening Standard *hired a room to do an interview. This press agent was a Scot and he kept saying, "Don't tell them too much because we're going to book the Sunday papers. We've got a story to tell." Then all of a sudden one of them said, "Why don't we go round Jimmy's?" Jimmy Murphy had a pub, the Jack the Ripper, in Spitalfields. So everyone decamped to there, all on free drinks.*

After we wound up, this Scots guy kept asking me if we were going to go. I said, "No, I'm busy. I ain't seen these people for two years, I want to have a drink."

All of a sudden the papers have come out with the story, and he's ripped the paper out of Jimmy's hand. I got hold of him. "These people are nice, don't do that!" Murphy would have fucking killed him. The Murphys were a boxing family, they weren't fools.

I was trying to be friendly with the guy. "Listen, calm down. Have a drink." He said, "Don't you ever fucking talk to me like that again!" This was all in the pub. It was ridiculous.

People like Tom Sargent of Justice[1] had said, "I think you

---

1 *Justice was the British section of the International Commission of Jurists. At that time it was arguing against the use of identification evidence as the sole criterion for conviction, with over fifty case files spanning the years 1973-5 that gave cause for "grave concern".*

should leave it to the authorities." But then, when George was released, he rang up and said, "Well done," so he'd changed his tune.

I just wish it hadn't been on the Queen's Prerogative though. I think the Home Secretary was leaving leeway there for us, as if to say, "Now get out there and prove your innocence." But George didn't want to know.

I'm sure we could have taken his case to the Court of Appeal. If we'd have carried on with the campaign, I think it would have come to that.

When I went to Scotland Yard and was introduced to the man who was going to head the enquiry into George's case, I took an instant dislike to him. I said, "I wouldn't trust you as far as I could throw you."

He sat there with his mouth open. I said, "I don't want Scotland Yard, I want an independent police force." So they brought in this Detective Chief Superintendent Mulder, who I had an awful lot of respect for. I get a feeling about people, and I thought the man was genuine.

DCS Mulder was from Hoddesdon, Hertfordshire; he was a great big man and his under-DC was called Graham. He used to say to me, "Let me do my job," which I had every confidence in. But whatever he did, I did too. He used to ring me up and say, "You've been there again, haven't you? You're very naughty." I'd tell him, "You do your job and I'll do what I've got to do." And he respected that.

I heard a couple of years later that he'd died from bowel cancer, but he did a good job. I think if George had been different, he would have helped him a lot more.

The day after he was released, George went on the telly with Ludovic Kennedy, who was a lovely man. I was trying to put words in his mouth before he went on, but he should have had his own opinion really. I said to him, "Now you've obviously got to get used to the fact that you're home. But we're going to fight . . ."

Peter said that to me the other day: "If only we'd have carried on with the campaign when he came out. He could have earned a fortune." He would have been the figurehead, because his name was already so connected with it.

But he went on telly and Kennedy put the questions to him. "I just want to get home to my wife and family and get on with my life," he said. Nothing else was mentioned.

RICK

I must have only been eleven that July. We went on holiday. The only times we'd been on holiday before that I can remember were when we went to Italy in 1972,[2] when I was only seven, and a long weekend in Spain in 1974. Now I thought we'd have a good holiday, but we went to Laysdown. I thought at least we'd have gone somewhere exotic. He borrowed a black cab and we drove down with Shirley and the kids.

I honestly thought that they'd pay him compensation for being in prison. After all, he'd gone to prison for something he didn't do. I thought he could somehow turn this around and make a few quid out of it, that they'd give him money for the story. He could have given his views on the criminal mind. He could have been a McVicar – who actually went to the same school as my dad, in the year above.

---

2 *Rose:* I took my mum to Italy in 1972. That was an experience. "Ain't a betting shop or a bit of bingo!" She went up to a traffic warden because he was dressed in white and asked for two cornets. She hated it. "I'll never come here again!" I said, "I'll never bring you!"

I thought we might all do alright out of it. Or at least go on holiday – not to Laysdown for two days.

He only once came up to the J.A.I.L. office in Upper Street, Islington. People like Ian Cameron, Martin Walker and David Milner had set up J.A.I.L., and I was a part of it too. But he didn't want to know. He was out now, he was being recognised, and that was that. I think I lost respect then.

I was still going to work, coming home and going to the meetings. But then I was becoming aware that I wasn't very well, what with the lump in my breast. I'd say to him, "We've got a meeting tonight."

"Oh, I ain't going to no meetings."

I couldn't believe it. I used to think, "How am I going to explain why he's not here?"

The ID laws up to that time were such that anyone could have accused you of doing something. If you had someone say, "Yeah, it was him," you were put away. The campaign and J.A.I.L. helped a lot of people. But then George let a lot of people down as well.

There was a case of a man being accused of conspiracy in Newcastle,[3] whose wife got in touch. Me and George went to the Law Courts and met the wife, but I don't think they released him. We were just there for moral support really, we didn't go to speak. We did speak on another couple of occasions, but that was under duress. He didn't really want to go.

---

3 *Raymond Turnbull was one of two men convicted at Newcastle Crown Court in October 1975 of what the prosecution described as a "bold and impudent" plot to rob a suburban bank. His conviction rested on a detective constable's ID, made from 62 yards.*

THE WARS OF ROSIE

CAMBRIDGE J. A. I. L.

Comments on the Devlin Report.

Cambridge JAIL gives the Devlin Report a qualified welcome. It is the first serious attempt to consider how the injustice created by the present law and procedure relating to identification evidence can be prevented. We welcome especially the official acknowledgement that "in cases which depend wholly or mainly on eye-witness evidence of identification there is a special risk of wrong conviction."

We agree with the following recommendations which seek to reduce this risk:

1. The judge must direct the jury to acquit an accused where the prosecution rests on identification evidence alone, except in certain exceptional circumstances.

2. The judge must direct the jury to acquit an accused where the prosecution rests mainly on identification evidence, unless there is a substantial evidence of another sort, except in certain exceptional circumstances.

3. The judge must direct the jury that where an alibi defence is put forward they must acquit the accused unless the prosecution can prove the the alibi is fabricated.

4. The police shall be required by law to observe the Home Office rules relating to identification parades and the showing of photographs to witnesses. If a breach of these rules affects the fairness of the identification the judge must rule inadmissible any evidence flowing from such a breach.

We consider that the Report has left judges too wide a discretion to define "the exceptional circumstances" mentioned in points 1 and 2 above. We accept that it is difficult to provide an exhaustive list, but we would limit the judges' discretion by providing that the following circumstances should not count as exceptional:

a) where the identifying witnesses happen to be police officers

b) where the accused does not go into the witness box to give evidence at the trial

c) where there are several witnesses who identify the accused

d) verbal admissions not made in the presence of the suspect's solicitor.

We feel that the Report does not seek to minimise the suffering imposed on the victim of mistaken identification. In particular, it does not do enough to prevent a person being charged solely on the basis of such evidence. We consider, therefore, that the police should not charge a suspect on the basis of identification alone, unless they have reason to believe that they will be able to produce at committal identification evidence of an exceptional nature or else substantial evidence of another kind.

We consider that all these points should be implemented by legislation as soon as possible. We welcome, in the meantime, the guideline governing prosecution in cases involving identification announced by the Attorney-General. These, however, should only be seen as an interim measure, especially since they do not cover points 1 to 4 above. We are also concerned lest the Court of Appeal's recent decision to set up a 5 judge court in July to consider a series of identification test cases should be seen as a substitute for legislation. The example of the unenforceable Judge's Rules should not be followed. Parliament must give the law to the judges and not leave it to them to create their own rules. As the Devlin Report says: "the discretion of the judge is the first instrument of tyranny. (para. 4.79)"

We go further than the Devlin Report in calling for the following points to be also included in legislation:

1. Identification parades must always be conducted in the presence of the suspect's solicitor and legal aid should be made available for this purpose.

2. Identification parades should be held at police stations unconnected with the officers investigating the case. All suspects in custody should have the right to have their identification parades held in prison.

3. Identification parades should be fully photographed.

4. Identification parades should be held as soon possible after the offence. Any delay should be accounted for by the investigating officers. If the delay is inordinate and unjustified any identification should not be admissible as evidence.

5. There should be no publicity connecting a suspect with an offence before an identification parade is held. Where there has been such publicity, any subsequent identification should not be admissible as evidence.

6. No witness should ever be allowed to identify an accused person for the first time in the dock of a court unless the accused, after consultation with his solicitor, has unreasonably refused to go on an identification parade.

7. Identification evidence based on a confrontation between suspect and witness should never be admitted.

We would also underline the need for every suspect to have the advice of a solicitor before and during police questioning and to be given the full reason for his arrest.

I said, "Look at all the people that have helped you," but he really wasn't interested. I would never have let it go. But then I thought, why should I carry on if he doesn't care?

GEORGE

They were doing the Devlin Report before I actually got nicked. I think it was down to George Ince and a guy called Laszlo, who were convicted on the wrong IDs.[4] It just happened that my case coincided with Devlin. We were hoping that it was going to be quite groundbreaking when it came out, but it was not on account of me, it was because of other people. There were certainly a lot of cases which were based on bad IDs.

I don't think the Devlin Report went far enough myself, but a lot of people begged to differ: "How far could it have gone?" Well, to be convicted solely on ID is wrong. How many people look alike? Years ago they all used to say I looked like Una Stubbs. I used to have my hair like her and people said I could be her double. I've looked at people on trains and thought, "Cor, doesn't that look like so-and-so?" How could you convict someone solely on the basis of how they look? It's wrong. I could have a beef with you and accuse you of something, and get one other person to say, "Yeah, it was him," and you're away. It could happen to anybody.

It was very sad really. A couple of times a week we used

---

4 *Laszlo Virag, a Hungarian immigrant, served five years in prison for wounding a police officer. Despite a credible alibi, he was convicted on the identification of eight eyewitnesses. In 1974, he walked free after his conviction was ruled unsafe and overturned.*

to go to the J.A.I.L. office and you'd have different people coming up there. I think it was a solicitor who allowed us to use his office. How many would do that for nothing, especially in Upper Street? It was an up and coming area then, it's very posh today.

Different people were coming in to Martin with their cases and we were just advising them how to go about it. I couldn't put a lot into it, they were the ones in charge. J.A.I.L. only lasted about another year, if that, and then everyone started getting on with their own lives.

GEORGE

It was alright when I was with my own family, but uncomfortable when there were all these people I didn't know. You've got to remember that there were a load of people who had been campaigning for me who were strangers. And they were all in my house when I got home. They were good people, they hadn't done any harm, all they'd done was work for me. But I didn't know these people. I didn't like the look of them.

Martin and the others had given up all their time. They were really dedicated. I didn't want to give up, because of what those people had done for me. Martin sat with me at the top of the Monument. We had to appear in court at Bank the next day. Martin stood with his hands in his overcoat and the clerk of the court said, "Take your hands out of your pockets!" "Fuck off!" said Martin in his really posh voice. He never paid any of his fines.

But the funniest thing that happened in the campaign was after we did the sit-down at Bethnal Green. We had to go before Harper Square magistrate's court, which is shut down

149

> **UNIVERSITY COLLEGE LONDON UNION**
>
> TELEPHONE:
> 01-387 3611
>
> 25 GORDON STREET
> LONDON, WC1H 0AH
>
> Aug 24th 1976.
>
> Please reply to
> Philip Engelman.
>
> Dear Rose + George,
>
> Enclosed are details of a conference on Prisoners Rights being organised by University College with the support of P.R.O.P. What we would very much like you both to do (either together or separately dosn't matter) is to lead a discussion group either on a specific issue or on a general topic on prison conditions. The idea behind the discussion groups is to generate some practical discussion on the reality of prison life in contrast to the theoretical aspects of the first part of the conference when the speakers have their say. We anticipate optimistically 20 groups with an optimum of 15 people, but of course it all depends on the turn out.
>
> We've also asked Lea + Albie, Ted Ward, Angela Singer of "Yorkshire Post", Pat Carlen of Brunel University, reps from the P.O.H., Prisoners wives, + families etc etc.

now. There was Colin, his wife, me and his two little boys. We all had our 'George Davis Is Innocent' T-shirts on. They said, "You can't take those children in with you." My brother said, "Where I go, my kids go!" "Matron will look after them."

Matron had them for all of five minutes. They kicked her, they bit her, and she soon brought them back. In the end they came in the dock with us. The magistrate said to each one of us, "What have you got to say?" Each one of us said, "George Davis is innocent." Even the kids said, "Our uncle's innocent."

UNIVERSITY COLLEGE LONDON UNION

TELEPHONE:
01-387 3611

25 GORDON STREET
LONDON, WC1H 0AH

University College London Union are sponsoring a Conference on Prisoners Rights to take place on Friday, 15th October in the Collegiate Theatre, 15. Gordon Street, London, WC1H 0AH.

The object of the Conference is to bring together all those concerned with our penal system, to discuss its problems and possible reforms that could be made to it.

The Conference is primarily directed at students, and its objective in relation to them are summarized in these motions passed at N.U.S. Conferences:

1) To actively support Prison Reform Groups;
2) To actively support such groups in their own areas;
3) In addition, the objective of the Conference is to bring an awareness to the student body of prison conditions.

It is further hoped that the wide spectrum of invitees will make the Conference as open and far reaching as possible. They are as follows:

1) Police Federation
2) Chairman of the Magistrates Federation
3) London Local Authorities containing prisons
4) Tom Sargent - Director of "Justice"
5) Howard Levinson - National Council for Civil Liberties
6) Louis Brom-Cooper Q.C., - Howard League for Penal Reform
7) Prison Officers Association
8) The Governors of the 5 London prisons
9) PROP
10) R.A.P.

The Conference will take the following form; there will be 5 topics for discussion:

1) Women in Prison
2) Health & Conditions in Prisons
3) Local Authority Roles
4) Censorship
5) Law

These will be presented by: Professor S. Cohen - Head of Sociology Dept., Sussex University

George Taylor - Chairman of the Plan ing Co., London Borough of Islington.
David Offenbach - Offenbach & Co.
John Platt-Mills. Q.C.
Mr. Kilroy-Silk. M.P.

The latter two await confirmation.
This will be followed by Workshops and finally concluded by discussion from the floor.

-2-

Specifically, the programme is:

10.30 a.m.	Start.
11.45 a.m.	Coffee Break.
12.00 p.m.	Workshops.
1.00 p.m.	Lunch Break.
2.00 p.m. - 4.30 p.m.	Open Forum.

The Press will be invited and the precedings of the Conference will be published, in order to ensure an on-going movement towards prison reform.

Enclosed are the briefs outlining the 5 areas of discussion. We will have ready on the day of the Conference, summaries of the main points of the various speakers.

Yours sincerely,

Philip Engelman

PHILIP ENGELMAN
President.

RICK

You have to understand that he'd been in prison all that time for something he didn't do. And he hadn't had a drink for a little while. I suppose being banged up for two fucking years is going to change you. But he definitely changed when he came out, he wasn't the same man as before he went in. He was the big fucking George Davis. That's how I saw it, anyway – he was a bit full of himself.

George suddenly loved the limelight, but he just wasn't like that before. I saw a change straight away. I saw it with girls when I'd be out with him. He was a face.

He became a celebrity really. But he was stupid. If he'd have only used his head, he could have earned a fortune. But he became the complete opposite to what he used to be – the man who always stood at the back in every photo.

When he became flash, he liked being recognised. It changed his whole outlook, because everywhere he went people recognised him. Since he came home he'd become a completely different person. He'd become a film star, a Mr Big.

Me, I used to cringe.

We went in a pub one night and were standing there waiting to be served. Because they weren't quick enough, I took the piss out of him. I banged on the bar. "Don't you know who he is? He wants a drink!" But he never told me to shut up.

Of course, when he was released, you couldn't expect him to come straight out and find a job. But as soon as I started mentioning it, oh no, he didn't want that. After a few weeks I started nagging him. It didn't look good, because he was still going in pubs all the time. He was becoming the biggest piss-artist God ever put on this earth.

He'd say, "I've got to see someone." In the life he was leading, the house was a hotel. I just let him do what he wanted, just thought, "Oh, get on with it."

If I'd say, "Where were you last night?", it'd be, "Oh, you're nutty, you! You talk a load of shit. You're imagining things!"

I knew I wasn't. I was getting too close to the truth. A woman's instinct is right nine times out of ten. "You're twisting things!" How many wives have heard that?

Deep down, I knew it was just going to be a matter of time. But I plodded along, as long as my home was clean and my Rick and Deana were alright.

I feel a little bit responsible for how he was when he came out. We made him something that he really wasn't, and he couldn't handle it. Can you imagine the boost it must have given him when he read the papers? We nearly always had something in there, even if it was only small.

And George never wanted responsibility. I was always doing everything – paying the bills, getting whatever we needed for indoors. So I do blame myself for a lot of it. I took on everything. It's my own fault really, but it's the way I am.

It was also around this time that I told George I'd found a lump in my breast. I'd left it and left it before finally telling him. He did insist, "You've got to go and get it sorted out."

I'd forgotten about myself because I had things to do. So, six weeks after he came out, I went in the London Hospital and had it removed. I can remember him coming in with Jeannie Ishmail. As usual, he said, "I can't stay long because I've got to meet someone."

Yeah, he had to meet his girlfriend. Like I say, he'd been home six weeks.

George was very nice to me when he'd written home from prison, but he was in a place where he couldn't do anything else. He couldn't slag me off, because I wouldn't have continued doing what I did. I laugh at those letters now though: "Can you get me this? Can you go around to so-and-so and get . . . And don't forget . . . Can you go round and . . . I've been in court all day, I'm absolutely shattered!"

I don't think I slept for two years. I'd go to bed and get a couple of hours, and if the phone went it was like I was on a spring.

PETER

When I came up out of solitary, after George was released, there was a prison warders' work-to-rule in the prison. This meant it was a virtual lockdown situation. The only time you were let out of your cell was to go along to the ablutions, clean your pot out and get fresh water. Nobody was getting exercise, there was no work. But during the work to rule, because it went on for so long, they started to let one wing out at a time. (I think there were about five or six wings in Walton.) What started to happen was that the lads had been incarcerated for so long that, when they came out, they sat down and refused to go back in. This normally only lasted for a couple of hours, but it was frustrating for the rest of the prison.

We were the last wing to get our exercise. When we went out, I'd only been off the block and out of punishment for a couple of days. As we were walking around, talking amongst ourselves, they spontaneously decided to have a sit-down. I joined in with them. The difference between our demonstration and the rest of them was that we didn't go back in. We stayed out there for six days, and at one point

it was down to maybe forty or fifty of us out of a wing of
two hundred.

This was during the summer of 1976's drought
conditions. They'd cut all the water supply off to the toilet
and the wash basins in the yard. The only water we were
able to get in those six days was from a stopcock in the
middle of the yard that was leaking. It was only a dribble
and we'd get a cup maybe every hour or so, which had to be
shared out among us. There were lads going down with
sunstroke and all sorts of things. The reason that we were
able to stay out in the yard that long was because the prison
warders worked to rule. They refused to carry out the
instructions of the governor.

There were a couple of funny incidents. One was when
they wanted to bring ice creams out to the prison warders
who were dotted around the ring. All the warders were
prepared to do on their work to rule was observe us, they
weren't prepared to get involved at all with the prisoners.
So the door opened to the wing and a couple of warders
came out with four boxes of ice creams that they were to
dish out. As they come down the steps and into the yard,
the lads walk up to them and relieve them of the ice creams.
We're sitting there eating them and they're all standing
about looking.

Another funny thing was that I'd seen the play before I
got my sentence and I remembered parts of it. During the
evenings, you'd have all the prisoners up in their cells
supplying us with tobacco, blankets or a sheet. But we were
also reading to them some snippets of the play. I had the
lads acting out the parts that I could remember. It was like
the Coliseum.

At one point the prison governor tried to get us to go back

*in. Davis had been released by this point, a week or so
before. The governor tried to drive a wedge between me and
all the other prisoners there. "We know that Peter
Chappell's the organiser of this." I fucking wasn't, it had
fuck-all to do with me, I just joined in with the rest of the
lads! "Don't listen to him, because he knows that he's going
to be released any day now that George Davis is out of
prison." That was a total fucking lie.*

*But the prison authorities made me the chief instigator,
the leader. So immediately after we came off the yard, they
shanghaied me and took me up to Durham prison, the
furthest prison in England from London. They kept me in
solitary all through the summer, for about four months. I
wasn't even allowed to exercise with anyone else. I could
touch both walls of the cell at once by spreading my arms,
that's how small it was.*

*I didn't think that way at the time, but now, on reflection,
I feel I was being treated as a political prisoner. They
definitely saw me as a threat because of the campaign, the
incident on the yard and my organisational abilities. That's
why they kept me up in Durham until about a fortnight
before Christmas, when they moved me down to Pentonville
prison for the last seven or eight weeks of my sentence. I was
treated really well by the warders and the hierarchy of the
prison down in London, with a lot of respect.*

*I went away on the sixth of January 1976, and came out
eventually on the seventeenth of February 1977, the
following year to George. It was a good thirteen months,
plus the remand period and all the other little sentences
when I was jailed for contempt. From the moment he was
arrested for the crime to the moment he was released was
twenty months. I probably did twenty months with all the*

other stretches of imprisonment before Headingley. So I did as much fucking bird as he did.

It felt wonderful to be out. I do remember worrying about how I was going to be received, in the sense of people's expectations of you. I think that when I came out I disappointed a lot of political activists, because they'd made a sort of career out of it, but I wasn't about that at all.

We knew when Peter was coming out, so I organised a big party for him in the White Swan. I sat up all night and made a net, blowing balloons into it, and put on a bit of food. It was good to have him home after all the rigmarole, and it went well. It was a good do. I don't know if things would have been different if Peter had been home when George was released. Perhaps he might have talked sense into him, who knows?

George was obviously pleased to see him home, but he didn't really make an effort to see much of Peter. Peter never ran George down, but I think he was disappointed with his response. My brothers were his brother-in-laws, so maybe he expected that of them.

Colin was very straight with him, he wouldn't mince his words: "What the fuck are you playing at?" On the couple of times they did meet afterwards, I know he had a few words. George wouldn't argue with Colin. I think by that stage, if Colin and Jimmy saw him in the pub they'd have a drink with him. But they sort of steered clear of him, stood back.

I don't know if it was hard for him to say thank you. But Peter wasn't family, and if I'd have had a friend like him I think I'd have kissed his boots.

George actually complained to me, after Peter came home: "You never had a party for me."

I said, "How could we have a party for you when we didn't know when you were coming out?" We didn't dance all night. We came home and lots of friends came over, but all I really wanted to do was to get rid of people. I was so tired.

But if the boot had been on the other foot, I don't think George would have been there fighting for me. I've often sat and wondered about how much of a shock to the system it would be if you'd never been in prison and someone gave you a twenty-year sentence. But then it was a shock to us all when he got nicked. He didn't see the hours going by till one or two o'clock in the morning, and the day starting again at six.

PETER

George never came round my house once. The only contact I had with him was on the day I got out. They had a big party for me at the White Swan in Commercial Road, all the media were there, all the local East Enders and campaigners. But I just spent the whole evening sat down with Shirley. I could have got into the swing of it, got myself pissed with all the gangsters, like George did on the day he was released. But I was different.

It wasn't a conscious slight, I just wanted to be with my wife. I wasn't a villain like they were. I'm not saying I was fucking whiter than white, given how I started my old business. But it was all working on my own, I never held guns to people's heads.

After I got out I kept well clear of Charlie Lowe. I never had a drink with him. I never had a drink with George. I never had a drink with any of them. I kept well clear of them.

I used to say to him, "Why don't you get a job?"

"You get your money, your social security."

I thought, no. *No.* I had a bit of pride. So I came off the dole and got myself a job in the Captain's Cabin, at St Catherine's Dock. (It's not there now, it's been pulled down.) I had a good job actually, with a lovely manager and good tips. But I worked hard, till the early hours of the morning.

One of my governors offered him a job. But no. "I ain't being a fucking wine waiter!"

"It's a job!" But he wouldn't work, it was beneath him.

RICK

I can remember him just going out on the piss basically. He went on a bender for about eighteen months, or whatever it was. All he was doing was getting drunk, coming home, and they were having rows. But then, what was he going to do? I don't think he was wine waiter material, let's face it. Fucking hell! He'd just come out of doing all that time. Imagine! Everyone knew his face.

But everyone knew my face, and I had to face it. I would have taken a scrubbing job if that had shown I was willing to work. He said I was nagging him – I was only nagging him to get a job and support the family.

I'd only been at St Catherine's Dock about six weeks. I think I was serving a customer. Unbeknownst to me, a woman who'd been sat in there all day was a reporter. The loos were upstairs, and as I went up to the ladies' she followed me.

"Mrs. Davis?"

"Yeah?"

"Have you heard the news?"

"No. What news?"

"Your husband's been arrested."

Oh, I could have broken my heart.

7

BUILD 'EM UP AND KNOCK 'EM DOWN

I ended up on the front page of the *Daily Mail*. The earth could have opened up and swallowed me. I'd had no inkling whatsoever of what was going on.

I must have gone a terrible colour, as the governor went to get me a brandy. I couldn't stop shaking.

George had been arrested while working as a getaway driver.[1] How could he even have considered doing anything like that? What must he have been thinking?

---

1 *At 9:45am on the morning of Friday the twenty-third of September, 1977, five armed robbers in stocking masks alighted from a red Ford Transit van outside the Bank of Cyprus in Holloway Road, London N7. Only a couple of the raiders were armed with shotguns, but their assault on the bank was rapid. After a Securicor guard who had been making a weekly delivery of £56,000 was clubbed to the ground outside with a truncheon or pickaxe handle, one of the raiders began attacking a bullet-proof cashier's screen with a hammer. As the cashier cowered on the other side, however, a contingent of armed police who had been awaiting their moment stormed out from a decoy furniture van. In the brief confrontation that followed, five shots were exchanged, three of them fired by the robbers – although nobody was hit. When the five were all subdued by batons or bludgeons, police moved in to block the Transit from escaping with its backdoors flapping open. The driver turned out to be George Davis, who is alleged to have claimed on the spot that he was delivering parcels – though the weapons on the passenger seat told a different story. Mickey Ishmail, battered but conscious, was already under arrest at this point.*

All I was concerned about was my daughter, who was at home after a bad asthma attack, and that all my ironing was left airing on a clothes horse. (We didn't have tumble dryers then, and I wasn't on the phone at that point either.) I knew the police had probably been there, so I got a cab home.

Deana was eighteen, going on nineteen then. When I got home, she said, "Mum, the police were ever so nice. They looked all round but they didn't touch your washing. They weren't nasty to me." In fact, she said that when she couldn't stop shaking they'd made her a cup of tea, bless her.

But she was ill for a few days. It was back to square one again.

I went shopping and when I came back she had about three friends in the kitchen. They were blow-drying one another's hair. I just flipped. I pulled the hair dryer's plug out of the wall. "Now all get out!"

I never did a bit of housework for three or four days. The washing up was piling up. I was knocked for six. My doctor couldn't believe that I wouldn't take any tranquillisers. But it wasn't a breakdown, because I soon pulled myself together.

Deana had started courting a young chap and she brought her future mother-in-law around. The place was like a tip.

"We've come to take you out for a drink!"

A drink was the last thing on my mind, never having been a drinker.

"How could you have brought that woman in here?"

"Oh Mum, it ain't bad, it ain't dirty." The kids couldn't see it, but all I could think of were the unmade beds. I'd just been thinking, "What's the point?"

Then I just woke up one morning and said to myself,

Ilkley
W. Yorks

Dear Mrs Davies,

I was very moved by your interview on the BBC Nationwide programme. Your frankness in answering several questions was quite amazing; I can say little to help your situation except to say that hope you will have support from your friends which will enable you to achieve all you hope for your childres.

"Come on. Get up. Pull yourself together." It was like putting on a stiff upper lip.

Peter had come round and got me after they were arrested. He was obviously disappointed, but he wasn't rude to me or anything. "I've had the television people round, they want to do an interview."

I said, "Oh Peter, I can't face it again."

"You've got to do it," he said. He stressed that he didn't think it was my fault. So I did it, but I don't know how. I've never watched that interview.

I apologised to everyone. I had to. I didn't try to make excuses for him. As I said, "I feel let down, but you marry for better or worse, so as a wife I accept it." I went on a few programmes: *Nationwide*, then I did interviews with John Stapleton and Desmond Wilcox, Esther Rantzen's husband. My Colin did about three interviews, there was quite a bit of coverage.

I was ashamed. I felt guilty, like a traitor really. Peter said to me, "There's thousands of people who you don't realise have respect for you," as I'm sure there were. But I felt gutted for all those people that had helped us. George didn't think he owed anyone anything, least of all me. George only looked after George.

GEORGE

Without a shadow of a doubt we were ready-eyed.[2] *Someone grassed us, and the police were waiting for us.*

---

2 *As George has subsequently described it, a cameraman working either for the police or the newspapers was ideally positioned at a second-floor window opposite the bank. On Saturday the twenty-fourth of September 1977, the* Daily Express *ran a three-page photo exclusive beginning on the front cover, headlined 'The Trap'.*

They could have nicked us prior to that but they didn't, they wanted to make it provable. They tried to shoot Mick as well.[3]

We pleaded guilty and that should have given us a bit of help as regards the sentencing, albeit we were caught bang to rights. But there you are. I've found out since that we actually went down on the wrong charge. Bear in mind that the charge wasn't just robbery, it was robbing a certain lady[4] *of £56,000. But the police had changed the bags, there was only paper in there.*

PETER

The Bank of Cyprus robbery was photographed, either by the police or by the newspapers. Either way it was all set up. I'd gone to college that day, and while I was there the police came round to pick me up. They came to nick me. They took me to a police station in Essex, I think it was Hainault or Loughton, and put it to me that I'd done an armed robbery sometime in '73 or '74. The person making the accusation was Charlie Lowe.

One of the things that they were doing in this period was getting to known villains and turning them. Not only were

---

3 *Mickey Ishmail would make much of the fact that the police fired a shot at him, the bullet lodging in the butt of his shotgun (reputedly in too bad a condition to actually fire). Several moments earlier, however, panicking in the face of the police counterattack, Ishmail had grabbed an eighty-two-year-old bystander and tried to take him hostage at gunpoint. The shocked old man, Bill Harding, commented that it was the closest he felt he'd ever come to death. He was freed by an incensed passer-by, fifty-three-year-old Albert Carney, who jumped on Ishmail's back prior to one policeman opening fire and the others going in with their bludgeons.*

4 *Bank cashier Elpide Savlangos.*

they milking them for the robberies that they'd actually gone on and the people they'd actually worked with, they were furnishing the grass with details of other robberies and people they wanted to fit into a frame.

I wouldn't know one fucking end of a gun from another. The only time I've ever seen a gun was when I was seven years old in Valance Road, just after the war. The headmaster, blind as a bat, was looking for this silver gun. The lad in front of me passed the gun to me and I passed it back. That's the only time I've ever held one in my hand. As far as working with Charlie Lowe or Mickey or any other armed robber, it was fucking ridiculous.

GEORGE

There was a guy who we thought was a good suspect for setting us up. I'm not going to say who, because we don't really know. And it wouldn't make any difference. At the end of the day, I'm not going to do anything. You'd be mad, wouldn't you? I don't understand it when people go, "I'll kill that bastard!" What for, so you can go back to prison for some more? You've just been away for yonks – so you're gonna come out and do him? You'd be crackers.

PETER

Certain people on the Left at that time – Ian Cameron, Martin Walker and people like that – were looking at police activities and reckoned they either tried to implicate me in that robbery because they felt that I'd slunk by them and got away without being noticed, or they were trying to tarnish me and the campaign.

Soon after George was arrested, we immediately held a press conference round at my house. The Times, *the BBC and ITV were all there. We issued a statement defending our campaign. Rosie in particular was defending George, but I wasn't. I was defending the campaign.*

I was gutted, but I wasn't going to let my guard down and show it to anybody. For me, the important thing was the campaign and the people that came forward and helped me. My loyalty was to those people. What I wanted to say to them was that what we did was right, it was correct, it was principled. We were in the right and we were victorious. George had let his family down, he'd let his wife down, and he'd let all sorts of other people involved in different campaigns down. But as far as we were concerned what we did was right, and all the support was justified.

When he got done for the Bank of Cyprus she was still defending him. I was so far apart from them after that time that I knew nothing about him seeing another woman, or about Ishmail breaking up with his wife. No one ever came near me anymore. But I was deeply saddened and it hurts me that he came out and did what he did, and treated her the way he did.

I used to wear sunglasses. Once he'd done what he'd done, I was ashamed. Truthfully, I didn't want people to recognise me. I wouldn't go to the shops without my glasses on, I ruined my eyes.

I've thrown loads of letters I received during the campaign away, which I shouldn't have done really. There was both good and bad: "He's done this before!" and all that. People always had their opinions.

But after he got nicked for the Bank of Cyprus, people were bound to say he must have done it the first time.

How could I stick up for him? I probably would have said the same.

But how do you think I'd have felt if he'd been guilty in the first instance? Do you think Peter would have left his wife and kids for a man he hardly knew if he wasn't certain of his innocence? He was staunch because he'd seen him that morning.

I never knew what was going on when they were planning the Cyprus thing. I knew it was only a matter of time before he was going to get into trouble though. My old instincts told me that.

But I never thought he would have done that. I didn't think he would have gone and robbed a bank in a million years. I was never a gangster's wife.

And so I stopped defending him.

PETER

When Georgie came out of Albany, he was released into an absolute glare of amazing publicity. And this bloke thought he was a proper gangster. George was nothing – I don't mean as a human being, but as a villain. There were proper villains out there at the time – Tommy Hole was one of them. George must have known him, he'd been on the LEB case with him.

Tommy was a bit more laidback, a bit quieter, a bit more secretive. He kept his cards close to his chest, didn't brag or anything like that. But they were upfront, Ishmail and Davis. They revelled in the fact that the police were following them.

GEORGE

Me, Tommy Hole and a few others got done for hijacking three lorry loads of whiskey. That took place in 1973, but we never got nicked for it till 1977, when Charlie Lowe grassed us.[5] I think we went to trial in July 1977, and we got acquitted. Then we got nicked in September for the Bank of Cyprus. Charlie was already a supergrass. He'd started doing the honours in about 1975, because we knew he was a grass by then. But he had nothing to do with the Bank of Cyprus. Charlie was nicked by then, he was in custody.

PETER

So the story goes, they decided to do the Bank of Cyprus job on a particular Friday and for some reason or other decided not to go ahead with it. They put it off for a week. On the Monday after, they were in the pub run by Jimmy Sheehan, the solicitor, having a booze after time. This place has got the gangsters and the Robbery Squad in there, all boozing together. At one point during the night, one of these coppers says to him, "When are you going to try again, George?"

The problem with George, and a fucking bad problem, was that he'd be everyone's friend. And he felt important when he was around Ishmail. The campaign made him feel even more important when he came out, it just added to all that.

Ishmail definitely found one with him, and with Charlie Lowe, who was also among the company – but I think

---

5 *Rose:* George knew Charlie Lowe, but only through the crowd he was with. We all went to Spain in 1974 for a long weekend, and he happened to come with his wife and little girl. He reminded me of one of the things my mum always said: "Never trust anyone with a funny eye." I was waitressing at Plantation House and George came down on the Friday lunchtime, said we're all going to Majorca. I didn't ask any questions about where he'd got the money or whatever. There were quite a few of us that went, all couples with kids.

Charlie did have some bottle because he did draw away, and he could handle himself. He was a different type of person to George. But they were still both diabolically used by Ishmail. I'm sorry, but George was a weak character.

Any time there was a problem in the prison, I sent a letter off to every newspaper in London. If the prison authorities were getting onto him, I used to react to it all. But he never once, as far as I know, did a thing to defend himself.

Our massive campaign had made something of him that he wasn't. You could see it in some of those little photos that were taken that evening. He's got the faces all around him, and there's the old vodka and tonic in his hand. I shit people like that, all fucking day long!

They were amateurs. As far as armed robbers go, they weren't even in the minor league. Ishmail was a user. Derek Felstead was a straight-up, honest working man, worked for himself as a lorry driver. He was a big lump of a man and he could fight. After he got nicked for that robbery it absolutely changed him.[6] He became a very different man, but he stayed away from armed robbery after that. That was the first dishonest thing that bloke ever did in his life. Ishmail just used him, and Derek hated him for it.

When the campaign was going on, I'd be taking the girls up to the prison every single day. I'd be telling George and he'd be hearing about what I'd been doing. I'm fucking sure they thought I was a bit of a wally. They think the working man is a tosser. They've got no respect for him at

---

6 Derek Felstead was the raider who wielded the hammer at the cashier's screen during the Bank of Cyprus robbery. For his troubles he would receive a twelve-year sentence. The rest of Ishmail's team, Davis and Felstead aside, were Freddy Davis (no relation), Jimmy Briggs and Steve Smeeth.

all. This is why they use the violence they do, because if you had any respect for working people you wouldn't be pulling guns on them. To go on the pavement they have to lose respect for humanity, because they're prepared to use these tools, these weapons.

Ishmail was just a bully. Holding a gun to the head of an eighty-two-year-old man was about his mark. Came out of Canning Town and into Stepney, threatened people, apt to use a knife and things like that. I never saw it, but he apparently got his comeuppance. There are two or three stories of where he'd rubbed somebody up the wrong way and they'd given him a fucking good hiding.

Mickey was in a corner when he did that, wasn't he? I'm not saying it's right. I'd like to think he wouldn't have hurt that old boy, but how do I know? I never really saw that side of him.

I've often heard people say, "It was the company George was keeping, wasn't it?" No, I really won't have that. And I'll give him his due – he's never blamed it onto anyone else.

George liked Mickey. Mickey liked George. They got on really well. Obviously Mickey had a big influence on him, but I wouldn't blame Mickey for anything George did. I wouldn't blame anyone that he was associated with. No one twisted his arm.

I wasn't asking for the world. I wasn't asking him to go out and thieve for me, just to get a job.

But George doesn't want to be disliked. Maybe he just didn't want to be a weakling in front of the others.

Like I've always said, you couldn't make me do something I didn't want to do. You can't blame it onto other people, you've got to be responsible for your actions, accountable for what you do. The sad thing is that, along the way, he's mucked up other people's lives too.

Everyone's entitled to one mistake. And it must be awful to be accused of something that you haven't done. How many men are in prison, even today, that shouldn't be there?

But you don't go back for a second lot. Maybe he wanted that limelight. Perhaps, because we got married young, he felt that he'd missed out on life. I really don't know.

Still, no one put him in that car, did they? All I can say is that prison can't be as bad as they say, or they wouldn't keep going back. George had his three meals a day, and what worries he did have were taken off him.

Then he still had the cheek to say, "I was fitted up!" "Yeah," I said, "and I'm the Queen of Sheba!"

RICK

Maybe my father was too weak, and Ishmail told him, "Come on, George," and he's been easily led into doing something. By being with Ishmail he would have been Jack the Lad. I'm not making excuses for him. If you're a man you're a man. You have to accept your own responsibilities in life. I don't know, but that's probably how it happened.

He had that group of friends who he mixed with, they were all at it. Maybe Ishmail did use them. But they were all fully game.

Or maybe it was a case of, "They made me what I am, therefore that is what I am." You might blame the police for that, because if he hadn't have got nicked in the first instance then maybe he wouldn't have done what he did in the second. Because otherwise, how could you be so fucking stupid? Why be silly enough to go and do something that you'd already been accused of?

To be lucky enough to have a campaign, with everybody helping you, and then to go and do what he did, it just made a mockery of it all. If he only saw half of what we had to go through: everyone laughing at you because they thought he was guilty the first fucking time; people telling you that to your face.

Everyone knew you for something in your life which was great, and now they knew you for something else. People in pubs, who don't really know me, still say it now: "He did the first one, didn't he?" I think it's probably a natural response. It seemed like he'd cried wolf, so why wouldn't people think that? If you didn't know him and you didn't know the full ins and outs of the case, you'd say he probably did it.

But he never did the first one.

Jeannie had divorced Mickey by then. I think their divorce was through by the time they were all nicked.

He broke her jaw; he stabbed her in the leg. All very charming. She finished up in the London Hospital and I had to look after the kids. That was around the time George got the twenty years for Ilford.

I think she'd been trying to get out of the marriage for a long while, but when he did that it was the final straw. From then until George was released, she'd been going after a divorce.

Jeannie could see the signs, where I couldn't. If she knew he was going on the turn, she'd say to me, "I'll be going home," and I'd be left thinking, "What's upset him?" He could be the life and soul of the party, but you could say one word and he'd turn.

How can love turn on a sixpence? I think love is respect. And if you lose respect then love goes with it. If it ever *was* love.

To women that stay with these men who give them good hidings, I'm sorry, but all I can say is no. *No.* Never in a million years. But they must like it.

I liked Jeannie though. I got on with her. We were friends for quite a few years. Her daughters and my granddaughters are friends now, they still keep in touch.

But she tells people today that the reason I don't talk to her is because she knew about George's affair and never told me. It has nothing to do with that.

(She stabbed me in the back on a personal level. George knew about it because I told him. And if he sees her, he still goes, "Hello Jean!" That's another stab in the back.)

After Jeannie and Mickey split, there was a girl who tried to knock him down in Commercial Road, but she knocked two nuns down instead.[7] It was her younger sister who George was carrying on with, but Mickey was with someone else by then. So it was all part and parcel of the clan.

But as I said, Mickey was what he was, and you knew what Mickey was. But when someone's devious you never get to the bottom of them. Give me a thief any day against a liar.

I admire a good thief provided they don't hurt anyone. I think that, today, they're probably forced to go out and do what they do. (The government are robbing us left, right and centre, but they think they have a right to do it, don't they?)

Not that I'm glorifying it. Some girls love to be gangster's molls, to go out with a face – but that was never me. I only

---

7 *Prior to the Bank of Cyprus raid, Ishmail's ex-girlfriend mounted the curb in her car to drive it at him. While he received injuries to one arm and a knee, Sister Joan West required twenty stitches to her head and sustained a fractured leg. The spurned woman was sentenced to two years, despite her former lover adding in mitigation that he made her pregnant before going off with another woman.*

knew them as friends. Some women, of course – like that one from Kent[8] who married Ronnie Kray – even do it to get the name.

It didn't last much longer for George and me. He came home on a Tuesday, went to a party on the Friday where he met this girl. Of course, people knew. We had little snippets through the post, people trying to tell me. I had nasty letters too.

It was all out in the open. One of my nephews walked in a restaurant one night and he was in there with her. He went back and told my sister, I only wish my sister had told me.

But there again, I would have preferred to find out for myself. I'm not a Jeannie Ishmail. She accepted all Mickey's affairs, but to me, once that's done that's it. Finished.

It took four or five months before I honestly knew. But you know what he used to say: "You're going mad."

I've got friends who had pubs and they said, "We've seen it all, but he was one person you would never have thought would do it."

When he'd done the Bank of Cyprus, he was still carrying on with this girl. She'd been up to the police station. I knew right away – when I walked in and they saw me, it was something that the policeman said.

I only went to the police station once, then I never went near him any more until the committal. I got his socks, cut the toes and heels off, cut the crotch out of a pair of pants, cut up a lovely shirt and then walked in there with it all.

The CID had never met me up to this point. "Mrs Davis?"

"No, Elizabeth Taylor," I said. "Would you give my husband these clothes and tell him I forgot the rope."

---

8 *True crime author Kate Kray.*

"Rope?"

"Yeah, to hang his fucking self with!"

I could hear them all laughing.

Looking back now, the screws were always very respectful towards me. I can't say one of them was ever rude. But after he got nicked again, you saw pity in people's eyes then. I didn't want that.

No. I don't suffer pity.

When I got in there, he had the cheek to say to me, "Could you get me a radio? Could you get me some oranges?" I said, "Let your old tart fetch 'em in!"

He was shocked. He still tried to deny it. I don't think he ever admitted what he'd been doing.

I don't think he ever felt any guilt about it – not only towards me, but towards my kids. How could he do that?

Still, he's not on his own, is he? I think most men might have done it, under the circumstances. This girl knew all about him. She was a single girl and she went after him. He was a face, he was well known.

Which was what we'd done for him. She'd have stayed away otherwise, she wouldn't have wanted to know. She was another gangster's moll. But when he got fifteen years for the Bank of Cyprus, her actions spoke for her. These girls are not stayers, they're not marriage material.

RICK

To be truthful, with all the aggravation, him being on the piss and arguing with my mum all the time, I thought we were going to leave anyway. He'd already stayed out a couple of times, doing whatever. I was fucking relieved in the end. Not because he'd gone to prison, don't get me wrong – but because the arguing would stop. When he wasn't there it was quiet, and then when he came back it was like all fucking hell had broken loose.

When we went to visit him in Brixton, my mother just slated him while I sat there. What a fucking visit that was! You can imagine what she said to him, she was just going into one. I can't remember her exact words, but I remember thinking, "Fucking hell, I don't want to be here!" It was the last place I wanted to be.

But what could he say? I think we just got up and walked out after that. I shouldn't have been there though.

GEORGE

When we got nicked for the Bank of Cyprus, I think the screws were highly delighted. I bet they couldn't believe their luck. They weren't gloating but they'd say, "What? Are you fucking mad?" Basically, "Are you stupid?" I suppose even people who worked on the campaign must have actually thought, "Well, if he did that he must have done the other one." Even though we know it doesn't work out like that.

I could not get the anger out of me. I went in Brixton nick and picked a table up. With the size of me, the screws couldn't believe it. I don't know where I found the strength. I'm only a little fellah, but I threw the table at him!

The screws let me do it all, as if to say, he's taken the piss out of you, now have a little go back. They sort of shut their eyes to it.

But the screws all knew my business. When you find out that someone's been so deceitful it really cuts deep.

I let him have it. All the other poor sods on the visit were making out they weren't listening. But they must have heard because I was screaming.

He really didn't like it. "You mugged me off!"
Mugged him off? What had he done to me?

GEORGE

*I'll be quite frank, it was my fault. She never did anything
wrong. But Rose and I were okay, up until she found out
that I'd had a bird visit me. And that was it. The end of it.
Which I understand.*

*It was totally humiliating for her. A woman scorned. She
was humiliated in front of those fucking screws, and other
people. I didn't wish to do that to her, but men are fucking
weak and that's the simple truth. But then again I shouldn't
have done it.*

*I sent a letter to the girl and they sent it to Rose instead.
Very nice of them, very nicely done. Then I think one of the
screws grassed my brother, who brought the bird up to visit
me. So there were murders round my mother's house
between Rose, my parents and my brother, who she didn't
speak to anyway.*

*I destroyed her. She was still ready to fight for me up until
that time. She doesn't talk to me, and I understand why.*

I went to the Old Bailey on the day. I just had to.

When they brought them out I was sitting right up the
front of the public gallery. They were all handcuffed
together. All the boys were looking round, but he was the
only one looking at the judge. He couldn't face me.

I got up in that court and shouted: "Rob a bank? You
couldn't rob a piggy bank!" Of course, all the press knew
who it was. Derek Felstead's wife, who I'm still friends
with today, says that she doesn't remember me doing it.
She was numb, basically. But I did it alright, at the

31/1   -1 FEB 1978   G. DAVIS 83073
H.M.PRISON
BRIXTON
SW.2.

Dear Rose,

I had a letter today from my mum and she told me what had happened. You have again jumped to the wrong conclusion. My mum or dad knew nothing about my visit Saturday and they had no idea who was coming to see me. Also the reason for the visit was not what you obviously think. Harry also told me of your views, so for me to explain will obviously do no good. Whatever happens, you seem to always want to believe the worst of me. It seems no matter what I do, I am in the wrong. No one

2

ever seems to give me the benefit of the doubt. Harry said you were coming up this Saturday, well Rose, please don't start shouting as I have enough problems as it is. You can never know what state I am in and dont suppose you are bothered at the moment. Everybody seems to want to add to these and butt their nose's in my business. I have not had a minutes peace since I have been in here. Even before you were told about my affair, you kept having a go at me. I am supposed to give evidence in the morning, but the way I am feeling I dont think I will be able

3

to. The difference is, I will not only be letting myself down, but everyone else as well. Anyhow Rose, I hope you can keep your cool on Saturday and will keep an open mind. I dont suppose you will believe me when I do explain, but you could at least listen. Also I think you owe my mum and dad an apology as I swear to God they did not know who was visiting me. I will see you Saturday. Give Deana and Ricky my love. Look after yourself.

Love George
×××××

highest court in the land. Once again, I should have got six months.

But even after all that, welfare used to ring me up from the prison: "George said would you come and . . ."

I thought yeah, arseholes! Do I look like I've got 'idiot' written across my forehead? I don't think so. I think I knew right away that I wasn't going to hang around for fifteen years. Especially after that girl visited him.

I think I must have had the quickest divorce ever. They didn't even question me. I went to court for it and I think it shocked him. I think he thought I'd be waiting forever.

Yeah, I fucking would, wouldn't I?

I went in and I told him, "I've got a divorce." This was about two weeks after his sentencing. The divorce itself can't have taken any longer than six months. It was uncontested, and it didn't cost me anything because I got Legal Aid.

The girl he was carrying on with fell by the wayside too. Did he think a young girl was going to wait?

George kept writing to the kids, but I never visited him again. When he got sentenced to fifteen years, I thought, "Oh well, that's that." In fact his junior barrister at that time, David Whitehouse, said to me, "Go home and get on with your life."

That was short-lived. Deana told me she was pregnant then. I thought, "Oh blimey!" But that was a happy event, it couldn't have come at a better time, thinking back now.

She was nineteen then. A good girl. A lovely girl. But my daughter was very withdrawn – she was a lot like her father in that respect. I remember when I was divorcing George, and I was doing an interview with John Stapleton, who was a very nice fellah. "It's so sad how things have worked out," he said. When he came back with his cameraman, he said,

---

TELEPHONE: 01-790 4032/5

EDWARD FAIL, BRADSHAW & WATERSON

Solicitors
Commissioners for Oaths
and
Oaths & Acknowledgments British Columbia

G. C. YOUNG   G. R. BARTLETT
J. N. VOKES
J. A. P. NEALE, LL.B.

OUR REF AN/OT.

YOUR REF

402, Commercial Road,
Stepney,
London, E1 OLG

AND AT
16, FINSBURY SQUARE, LONDON, EC2A 1BS   (01-606 1827/9)

4th April, 1978.

Mrs. R. Davis,
59 Belton Way,
Bow,
London, E.3.

Dear Mrs. Davis,

     As you are aware your husband's trial is pending at the Central Criminal Court and we expect to be given a fixed date of hearing in the very near future.

     We know that you wish to say a number of things on your husband's behalf and we feel that in order to put those matters together, it may be adviseable for you to come and see us at a time convenient to you.

     Mr. Richard DuCann Q.C., who is representing your husband would also like to see you and that would be in his Chambers at Queen Elizabeth Building, Temple, London, E.C.4. some time after 4.30, or if convenient to you after 5 o'clock.

     We should be grateful if you would be kind enough to contact us and let us know dates on which it would be convenient for you to call in to our office and also to attend Counsel in Chambers.

             Yours faithfully,
        EDWARD FAIL, BRADSHAW & WATERSON.

Edward Fail Ho

"Deana, would you mind if . . . ?", but she went, "No, I don't want my photo taken."

Deana wasn't a girl who would put herself forward. She was quietly spoken, but she wasn't a fool. She had quite a good job as a dental nurse at Moorgate, and they loved her where she worked. The dentist capped all Deana's teeth, it was a really beautiful job.

She loved it there, but when he got the fifteen years I think she was very embarrassed. Still, she stayed there till she had her first daughter.

My second granddaughter took me to the theatre recently. Afterwards, she said to me, "Nan, you have to let go!"

"What you don't understand, Lauren," I said to her, "is that Granddad had only been home a week when he found a girlfriend. Some women get the chance to get it all out in the open; I never had that chance because he was in the nick."

I was so angry, and I suppose I've never really let that anger go. Maybe Lauren will understand when she reads this.

8

AFTER
GEORGE

Some people became ill after the campaign; others saw their families go short. George has just got on with his life. I don't wish ill on anyone, not even him, but I don't think he's got a conscience.

I suppose a lot of people have held back about him because of Rick, my boy, which is only right. The sins of the fathers should not be visited upon the sons.

George came home the hero, but the heroes in my eyes were Peter and my brothers. I don't think Peter's seen him half a dozen times since he got out, if that.

It really did change Peter's life. He used to have that little van which he did deliveries in, and he was such a good family man. Shirley Chappell was one hundred percent behind us. But then Shirley knew what sort of person Peter was anyway, so she'd have been wasting her breath otherwise. Not many wives would have put up with it though, she had people traipsing through her place all day and night, the same as me.

She's now very ill, living on a nebuliser twenty-four hours a day. To see someone you know become so ill is hard. She can't do anything, and I understand her frustrations because I'm the same now. But she accepts it. She just says, "It's that emphysema again."

I still feel the guilt. I stopped going round there because I thought I was a reminder of everything that had happened. Peter could see the change not only in me, but in my kids. Plus I was busy working, weekdays and weekends.

I was invited to their daughter's wedding though, and I was glad I went. (They are a really lovely couple, though Peter is very militant. I don't talk politics with him!)

PETER

After the party that night, George never came near or rang me. Not a fucking word. Rosie never came near, nobody did for many, many years.

But the campaign was the best thing that ever happened to me. For somebody to come through a struggle like that, never mind being successful, is a wonderful experience. You couldn't buy that experience.

It happened a million times during the miners' strike and the printworkers' strike, those intensive struggles. The women in the miners' strike came upon an enormous freedom. It releases so much within the human being that it's very hard to go back to being just an ordinary person again. We live such boxed-in lives, and when you get into a struggle like that you break the chains.

Still, with or without Peter and all the rest, I would still have done something. I'm not saying it would have been as organised as they were, but I would have got something across. I would never have sat back and taken it.

There are some things I regret, but not a lot. I regret that

Peter had to leave his wife and kids, the same as my brother did. And all for what? How can you respect someone when they shit on you, like he did with Peter, Colin and Jimmy?

But as far as the campaign is concerned, I think it helped a lot of people and it did boost a lot of people who were in prison.

I tried to carry on with Martin and J.A.I.L. I thought George would have backed me. Of course, I was tired, I was going back to work then. But I couldn't let them down. And yet really, *he* should have been the one to do it. I should have been getting on with life and he should have been backing them.

RICK

Some of the people who came round home were frightening. Like 'Big H'. He always seemed strange to Deana and me, a bit odd. He was a quiet type, but he had a pilot's licence so he took Martin out in the plane. I could imagine him getting rid of Martin, dropping him off.

Him and his mate were supposed to be hitmen, killing for the money. They supposedly boiled up the bodies, kids too. When I heard it I thought, "Jesus, he's been round my house . . ."

J.A.I.L. was something that materialised in the latter part of the campaign. We intended continuing with that. That is how I met 'Big H', Harry MacKenney. He was a gentleman, he wouldn't swear in front of a woman. The biggest man I've ever met, but also one of the nicest men. He put a benefit on for us at his teddy bear factory.

Martin did a lot for him and his partner, so I suppose it

was his way of saying thank you. J.A.I.L. went to court for them, his mate had about three cases going on. I don't know if it was on robbery charges or whatever, but they got off.[1]

Big H played with my little granddaughter, Emma, after George had gone away again. He gave me a great big teddy bear for her. But as soon as I knew what he was supposed to have done, it went down the chute.

I couldn't believe it. As a person, you wouldn't have looked at him and said he could have murdered anyone. Well, I wouldn't have done, anyway. Harry was sent down for killing a dad and his little boy. That was a big shock. He did quite a few years before they said his conviction was unsafe and released him, which was not that long ago actually.

According to the bloke who confessed to it, that little boy cried to go with his dad. But his dad said, "No, you stay here." Of course, after he'd done the dad in, the boy had seen too much. It doesn't bear thinking about; he was only about nine.

It was terrible. Absolutely terrible.[2]

---

1 *Henry MacKenney hailed from the east London/Essex borderlands, and was arrested for two bank robberies in that region in December 1976. Charges against him were dropped when he compiled a detailed notice of alibi, but his business partner, Terry Pinfold, was convicted and sentenced to ten years. 'Big H' was adamant that this was a miscarriage of justice, so beginning his association with J.A.I.L.*

2 *At the end of the 1970s, Henry MacKenney and Terry Pinfold stood trial for their involvement in a series of contracted murders that allegedly spanned from the middle of the decade. The common factors were that none of the missing victims' bodies had been discovered, and all the details of the case were extracted from the confessions of John Childs, MacKenney's self-professed crime partner. Speculation as to how the victims were disposed of was acted out in court, when a forensic pathologist flayed a dead pig down to the bone and later destroyed its burnt remains with a hammer – as Childs claimed Big H had done.*

But Harry MacKenney was an absolute gentleman toward me. He came on a couple of the marches for George, and he even took me out for a couple of meals. Big H was a spotlessly clean man, always looked immaculate. He used to drive a little Mini, and as he was such a big man he looked a bit squashed in it.

Then look at that man Pat Cross. He did everything for his wife, but he went home and had a brainstorm. He murdered her.

Oh, she was a lovely girl. I only met her twice. And she had two little boys. It was tragic. George had been out a while then. I could *not* believe it when I read it in the paper.

Pat did time obviously. He wrote to me from Brixton while he was away.

Then one day there was a knock at the door. There was only me and my son indoors, and he was standing there with the two boys. Now what do you say?

I was in an awkward position so I invited him in. It was

It was enough to earn the defendants life sentences, with MacKenney convicted of four murders – including that of George Brett and his young son Terry, supposedly performed at a knockdown rate of £1800 for a personal enemy. According to the haunting testimony of Childs, Big H shot the father and son while the little boy was holding a teddy bear from the MacKenney factory for comfort.

Henry MacKenney's first appeal against his convictions was heard and overruled in 1981. His fight to overturn his sentence continued until 2003, when he and Pinfold had their convictions quashed. Both were now in their early seventies, with the formerly imposing Big H now frail and ailing. After twenty-three years, the Court of Appeal finally accepted that the confessions of the unstable supergrass Childs (who had also confessed to four murders not attributable to him) were an unsafe basis on which to convict. None of the missing persons named in the case has ever been found.

so sad for those two kids. I never questioned him, I just made him a coffee and said, "How's things?"

"Not too bad, Rose." He'd been let out on a weekend release.

He'd obviously had a breakdown. I believe the campaign had contributed to it. If we had meetings in the pub, at my house or around Peter's, he'd always be there. He'd be jotting things down in shorthand and he always managed to get something in the *Advertiser*, whether it was a big piece or a single column.

Pat Cross was a nice fellah. He did an awful lot for us and I'll always be grateful.

(Richard Madeley of *Richard and Judy* had his first job on the *Advertiser*, at the same time that Pat was there. He went to Cooper's College too, the same as George.)

Jeannie Murray got murdered too. She was courting Mickey Ishmail, came out of Hoxton. A lovely looking girl. Apparently she got a phone call telling her to go to Mickey's mum, who lived in the next block to me. Going up the stairwell she was knifed.

She'd changed her surname to Ishmail and her first name was Jean. They went into the prison the next day to tell Mickey, and at first he thought she was his ex-wife.

I came home and the police were everywhere. They knocked at my door, not that they suspected me or anything like that, they just interviewed everyone who knew her. They never got anyone for it, but me and my friends have got our suspicions.[3]

---

3 *The prime suspect for the murder of Jeannie Murray was briefly a taxi driver named Brindle – by a macabre coincidence, he was the ex-husband of an ex-girlfriend of Mickey Ishmail. Tried and acquitted of the crime, it is believed that he emigrated to a new life in Australia after he was exonerated.*

THE WARS OF ROSIE

So many things have happened, so many people have died, like Geri, the American girl. She did a lot for us. She did time as well – I visited her at Risley Remand Centre, it was a truly horrible place. This was a girl who didn't even know George, and as far as I know she'd never been in prison. She was very politically minded, and she was driven by the sense of injustice.

The people he was involved with were all nice fellahs – I'm not talking about the criminal side of their lives – but nearly all of them are dead now. Tommy Hole got shot in a pub at Beckton a few years ago. He walked in the pub one Sunday lunchtime, him and another fellah were drinking at the bar, and someone walked in and shot both of them.[4] That was terrible.

If you met Tommy, he was really nice from a woman's point of view. But his father committed suicide, his son committed suicide and he got shot.

Young Tommy only had about six weeks to do of a prison sentence.[5] He was a lovely kid, I find it so sad. I don't know how his poor mum can have taken it.

---

4 *Tommy Hole and Joey Evans were the victims of balaclava-clad killers at the Beckton Arms in December 1999. Speculative motives for the double hit include short-changing the buyers on a major drug deal and Hole's reputed involvement in the gangland murder of notorious hitman Nicky Gerard. Hole stood trial for the killing of Gerard (son of the equally infamous Alfie, a hired killer for the Krays) back in 1983. The prosecution relied solely on identification evidence which led the judge, post-Devlin Report, to dismiss the case.*

5 *Young Tommy Hole died by hanging in 1991. Tommy senior and Tommy junior were occupying adjacent cells at the time, so interlocked were their lives. Rumoured motives include a prison drug deal gone sour. Young Tommy apparently seemed unnaturally light-hearted on the night he committed suicide.*

But then it's amazing what people can take really, isn't it? George England has died of cancer. Mickey Ishmail died in France a few years back. None of these people are around any more.

When Prince Charles said that phrase, "whatever love means," when he was getting engaged to Diana, I thought, "You stupid bastard! Fancy saying that!"

But he was right. What *does* love mean? You get men lusting after women, but that's not love, is it?

It's a rare thing. How many couples now stay together? A friend of mine's daughter had a beautiful wedding, it cost thousands. Six months later they were divorcing. Is that *love*?

I think you can be fond of someone. But it's like when a mother says, "I love my son, but I don't *like* him," it's that sort of contradiction.

After me and George divorced, I certainly wasn't a nun. In fact, I would say I went to the opposite extreme of what I'm really like as a person. I saw quite a bit of life. I had a couple of friends, bloody good friends, and I'd go out every week if I wanted to. And I need never have been on my own.

But then they got too serious, and I would never have got married again. Never in a million years. I would never wait on another man as long as I lived – only my son. I think it's turned into a protective thing with me.

I've had some good times and some wonderful holidays. I met someone who was quite wealthy. I needn't have worked again – but no. We had some laughs and we're still friends today. I could ring him up and he'd be there for me. (He's married now. I know his wife.) But I was quite contented now to have my own space.

George's mum and dad stuck up for him – which was only natural. They were lost for words at first, but they were very quiet people anyway. My mum used to say, "George's mother's a lady." She very rarely swore, whereas my mum was the complete opposite.

(If my dad had been alive, the shock of what George had done would have killed him. He thought he was such a gentleman, he would never have believed it.)

I think they went into a shell because of the shame of it, though having the grandchildren gave them something to live for really. They were getting on by then, into their sixties, though George's dad was still at work. They didn't need friends because they were so devoted to one another.

I had good in-laws. George came from a lovely family, and that's what's so sad.

If it had been one of my brothers, I wouldn't have been shocked – not that they were villains, but a couple of them were lairy. Colin was always fighting after having a drink. That man could have a fight, as could Jimmy.

My mother-in-law never really said a lot, but you could sense what she was thinking. In her eyes George never grew up. He was still her little boy, and she was very protective of him.

I still kept in touch with them, and the family in general, even after we divorced. My mother-in-law had a heart of gold. My kids wanted for nothing – whether it was clothes or whatever else. They loved their nan and granddad, and my mother- and father-in-law worshipped the ground that Deana and Rick walked on (though Deana always got that little bit more at Christmastime). His aunt was still a good friend too. If I was short of money, I could still knock there and she never refused me.

Even today, if any functions or events go on in the family I always get an invitation. So I can't have been that bad a daughter-in-law, can I?

Of course, I still had my home and my kids to keep – admittedly they weren't babies, but then Rick went through a really funny phase.

Him and another boy got accused of kicking in a window. But he told me, "Mum, honestly, I never done it," and I believed him. We had to go up to the police station, so I said I'd meet him there after school. As I got off the train from work, him and this other boy, who supposedly smashed the window, didn't see me walking into the station. They were skylarking about.

I walked up to Rick and fetched him one.

"What was that for?"

"Don't stand in the police station laughing! There's nothing to laugh at!"

We had to go to the new court in Bow Road. This copper got up and said that he'd seen him kick in the window with his brown boots.

I screamed out, "He don't even possess a pair of brown boots!"

Rick got bound over to keep the peace. "Thanks for bringing this worry on me," I told him.

I ran the other boy all the way up Bow Common Lane. I said, "If I see you with him, I'll go round to your mum and dad!" Rick told me afterwards, "He don't go to my school, he goes to work." I did feel a bit of a fool.

Still, I took Ricky over to my brother in south London. I said to Colin, "I can't cope with him." "Mum, I don't want to stay!" moaned Rick. But I said, "You'd better stay here for as long as it takes." It broke my heart to leave him there. He was only twelve.

My Colin was living along the Old Kent Road, and you can't get a lot rougher than that. Him and my Rick loved each other. He had a way with kids. He left four lovely sons who still call me 'Aunt' now that they're men, they're very respectful.

Colin helped the church a lot with underprivileged kids and pensioners. Every year they used to take the kids away and he would go with them to do all the cooking. One year the priest, Father Owen, said to him, "We won't be able to do it, the money's not there." So Colin did a sponsored twenty-four-hour bike ride and raised £1,000. That was a lot of money then. He had a lot of goodness in him.

I left Rick there for a month. I'd go over there to take a bit of shopping and he'd say, "Oh Mum, I want to come home!"

"No, not until you sort yourself out."

And he did. He was an angel as a little boy, but he needed a father around. He went off the rails a bit, though his school were wonderful about it – they even got him a job at Poplar Town Hall, which later went fulltime when he left school. It was all part of growing up. You have to accept that, but as they get older they've got to get wiser.

Still, can you imagine what all of this was like to a kid? I know what it did to me; I can never be sure about Rick. People were fighting to get his father out; he was on the telly; he was so proud. One minute it was all elation, then the next – *crash, bang, wallop!*

When I had my problems with George, to give my family their dues they were all there for me. They were staunch.

But I get quite upset sometimes when I sit and think about my mother. When I got on my feet I could have helped her. But she went senile and that's what's sad. She didn't know what was going on anymore.

She'd brought up a big family, worked bloody hard for us, and then she found herself on her own. That must be really hard – I understand it now because I'm on my own too.

But then I think sometimes, "What am I complaining about?" My mum had loads of us kids. Can you imagine having a full house and then they've all flown the nest and you're left redundant?

And then her poor mind went. My mum first started

getting the dementia in her middle seventies, which must have been in the early 1980s.

I'd rowed with my family over George – sticking up for him, believe it or not.

But then they put my poor mum in a home, God rest her soul. We should have all got together and discussed what was going to happen to her. My two sisters decided on it, but it was a neighbour who pulled me up in the street and told me. I could never forgive them. I just stopped talking to all of them.

I still had a home to run, and I'd gone back to working banquets at St Catherine's Dock. So if I was going to work in the evenings, I'd pop to my mum's for the couple of hours I had in the break. I tried to see her at least once, twice a week. But if I was busy, then I couldn't.

When my dad died, I'd had my mum stay with me for three months. I was the only one that ever took her abroad. But because my mum lived so near to my sisters, one would do her windows, one would clean, one would cook, one would make sure my mum was bathed. They looked after her.

But my mum wasn't used to everything being spick and span – she would flick her ash anywhere, she'd kick her shoes off and there would be newspapers everywhere. I used to wonder if they were doing it because people knew that's where their mum lived, and because they were so house-proud that they thought people would talk about them if they didn't.

I went up there one day in between jobs and my sister Doreen (who later died) came up with my mum's dinner, all in a lovely tablecloth. My mum was going senile then. "Oh," Doreen said in a superior tone of voice, "what are *you* doing here?"

We had a terrible fight. I can see my mum now, getting up from the table. "*Oh, don't, don't!*" My sister was very soft, and she started crying. "I'm going to get Malcolm!" – he was a lovely man, the one who made me the doll's house. I said, "Go and get who you bloody want, I'll still be here till five o'clock!" I never spoke to either of my sisters again.

But that's life, I suppose, isn't it?

I never even followed my mum's funeral car when she died. I went to the funeral, but I didn't ride with my family. I couldn't. After she'd fought hammer and tongs to bring us all up, how could they put her in a home?

I'm not saying she wouldn't have finished up there eventually anyway, because she really didn't know what she was doing. They'd put bells on her slippers because she'd got out of the old people's home. The police found her in Bromley-by-Bow and the home was in Bethnal Green. She must have crossed main roads to get there.

She was a good old girl. I often think of her, and a lot of her words and old sayings come back and ring true.

Back then though I just thought, "Sod it." I had to put everything behind me and just get on with my life. I went after a wine waitress job I saw advertised in the paper. I've always been very confident at interviews. The employer was showing me all around, telling me what my duties would be.

"When can you start?"

"I can start Monday." This was the middle of the week, probably Wednesday.

"Fine."

But after I'd filled the application form in, as soon as he'd seen the name he said, "You're not *the* Rose Davis?" I said yeah. "Oh," he said, "I'll be getting in touch."

They wrote me a letter to very politely say that someone

else had already been employed and he hadn't known about it. But of course it was because of who I was.

I was taken aback by the reaction to the name. I hadn't done anything. I hadn't been nicked for robbery or thieving. I've never even been sacked from a job – though I've walked out of jobs on principle.

So I was working casually then at Whitbread's, and I asked one of the managers if I could be considered if a job came up. They came up with this job where I would work with the two butlers who attended the chairman.

Paul, one of the butlers, was a lovely fellah. The head butler thought his shit didn't stink. I used to be in there at half past six in the morning and finish at three. But then on some nights the chairman used to entertain, perhaps twice a month, which wasn't too bad.

One morning when I'd got up a bit late, the head butler said, "Could you do those back stairs now?"

I said, "Robert, put a broom up my arse and I'll sweep the passage as I go along."

"Now there's no need for that!"

I was at Whitbread's for nearly twenty years – even when I had another job, I used to go back there at nights and do banquets. I worked on the top table with my partner Cathy, a little Irish girl, for about ten years, and I served people I never thought I'd ever meet. I served drinks to Prince Charles, I served Princess Anne a couple of times, Maggie Thatcher, Princess Margaret – who was an absolute *pig*! She didn't say a word, she dismissed you with her hand, and smoked continually with no consideration for people eating around her. Robert said to me, "Rose, when the Queen Mother comes out of the lift, you have to curtsey." I looked at him and said, "Robert, I'm not ignorant." I did know my etiquette. But if it happened today, I *could not* curtsey to Camilla Parker-Bowles out of principle.

I served quite a lot of stars; I enjoyed Whitbread's. I won an award for excellence in service at a do at the Park Lane Hotel. I took Deana with me. When they called me out I was so *embarrassed*.

I had a manager who was brilliant, called Steve Tarbuck. He went there when he was young, as a cook, and had a bad accident. It did something to his eye, so he had to come out of the kitchen. All the girls taught him how to lay tables, how to do Silver Service. He worked himself up the ladder to management, and he was always very fair with me and the other girls. When there was a top job coming up, he went after it but never got it because he didn't talk with a plum in his mouth. It was so sad, because he'd worked there for twenty-five or thirty years. He put his heart and soul into that job, but when he left there he sent for a job reference, and they couldn't even remember him.

I cleaned for one of my managers and his wife for seven years. They were *posh* with a capital 'P'. But I thought that man didn't know who I was, as I'd changed my name back.

One afternoon he said, "We'd like to take you to the Ritz."

"Ooh, me at the Ritz!" I was joking with him.

When we got there for afternoon tea, he folded one leg across the other and said, "So, who did all that painting: 'George Davis Is Innocent'?"

"I didn't even know you knew, Mr Melvin."

"Of course I knew!"

"And you trusted me in your house?"

"I certainly did!" He just laughed at me.

I didn't want my kids to side with me over George, because he was their dad. They had to make their own minds up. Deana held everything in, as she always did. But then later, in the end, I think it all came out. (Not that he'd ever accept the blame for that.)

That girl used to take her two kids – she had her second in the early 1980s – to all the different prisons, it was a bloody hard slog. I'll never know the extent of the strain that placed on her.

RICK

I didn't go to visit my dad for a few years. I'd write to him sometimes. I think he ended up doing six or seven years. When he got nicked for that first one, he said he was never going away again. He was only at home for eighteen months.

When he was finishing off his sentence, he did about three or four years in Maidstone. Me and Deana used to visit him there. They've got an outside swimming pool, he quite liked it down there. They'd all been Category A – I think it was double-A at one time – but when he got down to Maidstone it was a bit easier. I suppose he was settled, and Derek Felstead was there with him. (Ishmail had been shipped off up to Durham or somewhere.) There were a lot of people in there who he knew or made friends with.

I don't think he became institutionalised, because I don't think he liked it that much in there. I suppose he just got on with it. No one wants to be in prison, but you're there, they're not going to let you out, so you've just got to buckle down.

GEORGE

It was fifteen years and then we got it cut down to eleven on appeal. I was very fortunate, because I was informed by the barrister that if you go to appeal, everything you write down has to be read by the appeal judge. When you're in prison you get what they call FG forms, 'further grounds'. At every prison I went to, I'd find someone who got a lesser sentence than me and got away with the money – because we never got away with anything. "How long you doing? Nine? You got away with the money?" I used to write down all the details and just keep sending the forms off, driving the judge fucking mad. I don't know whether that worked, but as I say, we got it down to eleven – what they called the irreducible minimum for bank robbery.

They set the tariff for one bank robbery at fifteen years, which was for pleading not guilty, I assume. For subsequent bank robberies it went up to eighteen and twenty-one. They've got to give you credit for pleading guilty, which hadn't happened with us initially.

But a few years into our sentence, when we were at Albany, three black boys got done for a bank robbery. They took photographs of them, someone grassed them and they got nicked. They all pleaded guilty, but they got away with the money: one got five, one got six, one got seven. How does that work out?

My sentence was boring. Bear in mind that I'd got used to it by now. Even though I'd only done the two years, I'd done it as a Category A prisoner. So I was completely aware of what to do and what would happen.

When I originally got the fifteen years, the best I could hope for was to get out at halfway. Then when my appeal was granted and I got it cut down, the most I could do was seven and a half, so what had been the best possibility now became the worst, which was good. Mind you, they nearly made me do all of that – but it could have been a lot worse, bearing in mind how they'd been humiliated by the campaign for me.

When George came home I offered to let him have the maisonette, provided he took on my boy with it, who was grown up by then. He didn't want it.

He went to live with his aunt, didn't want any responsibility. I could have walked away at any time, but my kids came first. That's the only thing I regret – for two years of my life, I didn't really have them.

He even committed other crimes when he came home after the Bank of Cyprus. He's been back inside since for robbing trains[6] – not on his own, but with someone else apparently. I'd have come home and been a choirboy, I think.

RICK

I knew what he was up to. I knew what he was doing at the time, and I obviously didn't want to see him go back to prison, but I couldn't tell him not to do it. He was a grown man. I just hoped he didn't get caught. I thought, "Well, at the end of the day, he's not armed, it's not as heavy."

Dad met this bloke in prison who could open the cages to the registered mail. So what they'd do is dress up as policemen; go on the train; move right the way through the carriages, making sure that there were no Old Bill on there. Then my dad would stand at the door. He'd go in, open the cage, clock the different colours that they had for the registered mail, then put it all in a bag. If anyone came in, my dad had a fake warrant card. He'd say, "Sorry, police!" and they'd go.

---

6 *In January 1987, George Davis and John Gravell were sentenced in connection with an attempted raid on the London to Brighton mail train in March of the previous year. As George admits, this was the final event in what had become a regular routine. Rick Davis gives details of the caper above.*

They only got caught when the bloke he was doing it with took the envelopes and stuff down to a dump. He'd go and do it maybe once, twice a week, and another bloke had seen him do it.

This other bloke has gone through the bag to see what he'd dumped. Of course, it was all letters that had been opened. He took his number plate, informed the police. So when they went out on this one night, the Old Bill knew what they were planning and followed them. Bosh! – my dad got caught. He held the door and the other bloke got away. They've gone running through the train. He's pulled a knife out and stabbed a policeman, but it's gone through his coat. He's pulled the emergency cord and jumped off. He beats the Old Bill back to his house and goes on the run.

He wound up getting ten years. He had the hump over the fact that my dad only got eighteen months. Well, the fact is that Dad would never have got caught if it hadn't been for him. And then he tried to stab Old Bill . . .

They pushed it through as if my dad was there all the time, but there's a lot of things he didn't do. I met the other bloke, gave him my dad's statement while he was on the run. The silly bastard, they caught him at his daughter's twenty-first birthday party. "Lovely, thank you!"

Dad did seven or eight months for that in Wandsworth. He said that was his last. It was the hardest bit of bird he'd ever done. He realised, "I've had enough of this game, I'm getting too old for it." Wandsworth is well tough. He said how scummy the people were, because it's a lower cat. With a Category A prison, you tend to be among a higher class of prisoners generally. I'm not talking about rapists and nonces, but people doing long terms who are a bit more sensible, if you like. In a short-term prison you get smackos and the whole shit-scum barrel of dogs.

I remember when Mickey Ishmail came out. This was around when my dad had come out for the second time after the Bank of Cyprus. I was that much older then, in my twenties, and I hadn't seen Ishmail for years. He'd done other bird, he went away for an amphetamine factory. This chemist said that he'd been forced to make drugs for Mickey – Mickey put a gun to his head. That was after they got caught. The chemist still got bird, I think he got about five. I went into the court to watch the case a couple of times. Mickey got a lump of bird, seven or nine.

Ishmail came round for us to have a drink with him and Marilyn, his girlfriend. I went and played pool with him in a pub. He said, "Play for money." So we had a tenner on it, when a tenner was a lot of money. Then he lost, and he did not want to pay me. I went, "Come on, are you having a laugh? Give me the money!" I got it off him in the end, but if everyone hadn't have been there, or if it had been anyone else, I don't think he would have paid it.

I didn't like him. He was a manipulator, a control freak. He took up with a few women, had a few kids by different bits and pieces. But he made this girl, Marilyn, into a bag of fucking nerves. She was skinny, and she'd shake.

George doesn't live in the East End anymore. He lives in north London, at Highgate. He's got a new circle of friends, but they'll never be friends like he used to have. They're acquaintances as far as I'm concerned.

When he came home again he found other girlfriends, and then he met Jenny who worked in the Ritz casino – who was quite nice, had never been married and had her own flat. I always said that if he fell in shit he'd come up smelling of roses.

Her father was a commander in the police force. I did say to her once, "I wonder what your dad would make of this?" She said, "I bet he's turning over in his grave." She talks ever so nicely, but I think the name 'George Davis' was the attraction, it gave him a sort of charisma. I think he's proud of himself. I'd want to hide under a stone.

She still works in a casino, she's like a *maitre d'* there. George takes her to and from work, he's a very good husband now. It's a pity he didn't do it for me – walking along Bow Common Lane at fucking twelve o'clock at night. I couldn't even afford a cab.

He's got on with his life, and good luck to him. I try not to say anything to my boy, I know it's wrong. But, if a couple break up under normal circumstances, you can have your row and get it out in the open. He was in prison, so I couldn't.

But I wouldn't waste my breath now. It's gone past that.

I was earning decent money myself by then, so I moved out of my old maisonette in '89. I loved living there, it was a lovely little estate but now it's terrible. The walk along Bow Common Lane to Mile End is horrible too.

I worked with a waitress who told me that the young girl facing where she lived wanted to do a tenancy exchange. So I brought her over to see the maisonette. She said, "Ooh yeah," then she changed her mind. But then I went to see a fortune teller, and he said, "You are going to move." The next morning I got a phone call from this girl. She said, "I'm sorry I messed you about, but I will come with you to the offices and we'll do an exchange." I'd hung all the curtains and had the place carpeted, so I thought I'd treat her, and I paid all her rent up before she moved in. But she only lived in my place for a year before she committed suicide. She was a lovely looking girl, but she obviously had problems. Her mum and dad lived next door, they were elderly and they've both since died.

I moved into my new two-bedroom house at Stepney Green with an armchair, a telly, a bed, a fridge and a cooker. All I've got is what I've worked for. My boy would live with me there until he got married.

As I walked out of my old flat and shut the door, I never even looked back. It's weird, isn't it? I was there for over twenty-five years.

9

DEANA

I'd been talking to my neighbour over the road, and she got me an interview for a job as a housekeeper. By then I'd reverted back to my maiden name. I got the rent book changed to Dean, so I never used the name Davis ever again. My employers at Whitbread gave me an impeccable reference. But when I got the form, it asked for both married name and maiden name. So I put my nan's name, Barker, as my single name and Dean as my married name. The bank obviously didn't check very well, but that's neither here nor there now. I worked there for over eleven years

I loved that job. I had the keys to the flats that I cleaned, and I'm talking about million-pound flats. I was my own boss. I looked after one of the bank's flats for about a year, and then they bought another in the block over at Bryanston Square – it was nothing to see Rolls-Royces pulling up, it was only the senior banking staff who stayed there. I took Deana in a couple of times when I was really busy and gave her £40 for helping me. I'd never let her do heavy stuff, just a bit of dusting and ironing or whatever.

I looked after a couple of lords and ladies up there. Lord

Sainsbury lived in the block – he was a gentleman, he used to open the door for me.

I had a couple of saucy ones that I chucked out too, I didn't take any shit! One fellah came back with a bird, which wasn't allowed in the hospitality flats. I told him, "You took liberties, now get her out of here." He went out and left his bathwater in. I ran up to him at the lift. "'Ere, I don't clear your shit up!" When I rang my governor he agreed I should chuck him out. I had all his things packed when he came back.

I went in there one day and a man had left me a £100 tip for cleaning his room and doing a bit of laundry. They were all bank managers earning fabulous money. It was nothing to walk into a room where there would be a thank-you note with £40 in there.

But in the year of the plane bombings in America, as it was an American bank we were all made redundant. The bank is still going today, but they got rid of the flats. I was sad to leave there, but it was far from the worst thing that happened that year.

It was back in the mid-1990s, when I'd taken my granddaughters to America as a treat, that Deana was first diagnosed. While we were out there she was having tests. I rang her up, and when I think back now it must have sounded terrible. But that's how I am.

Of course there's a time difference, so I rang at one o'clock in the morning.

"How did you get on?"

She started crying. "It's breast cancer . . ."

"Pull yourself together," I said, "you've got two kids!" I didn't express sympathy with her at all, because I knew that if I did I'd go down.

"Oh Mum, what's going to happen?"

"You know we'll get you sorted out. When I come back from America."

I had another eight days to go out there. You can imagine what was going through my mind.

Her eldest girl, Emma, said, "Nanny, how did Mummy get on?" I had to lie to her.

I can remember being in the pool with the little one, who was only seven or eight at the time. I said, "If you had a wish, Lauren, what would you wish for?"

"That Mummy's gonna be got better," she said. I'll never forget that.

Deana's friend at the time said to me that the way the doctor had broken it to her made her hysterical. So the first thing I did when I got home was make an appointment to see him.

His nurse was with him. "I understand you're concerned . . ."

"Can I just say that your bedside manner needs checking?"

"You can't . . ." the nurse tried to butt in.

"Mind your own business, I'm talking to the butcher not the block!"

He put his head down. I said, "Now I want the truth. What's her chances?"

"Thirty percent." Not bad, but not good.

Funnily enough, I'm under the same doctor now and I've got a lot of respect for him. But then I told him, "I want you to lie through your teeth. Tell her anything, but don't tell her how bad she is."

I went with her for her first lot of chemo. He said, "Come on Deana, you're *not* going to die." It took six weeks for them to find out about the lump she had. That's what gutted me. It was fifteen by twelve centimetres. Now that's big, like a small orange.

All that this lady house doctor had told Deana was to go home, see her doctor and get some Prozac. I went *mental*. I made an appointment and went up to that hospital, I was like a lunatic. The sister came out and said, "Please come into this room." I told her, "My daughter never complains, and when she came up here last time she said she had a pain. Alarm bells should have gone off."

They made an arrangement for me to go and meet this professor, her consultant, the next morning. There were all these people waiting at his clinic, and the receptionist said, "He can give you ten minutes." When I told him, he put his head in his hand and said, "Why didn't you bring her back here?" I said, "Back here? You've let her down!"

He asked me, "Who's she under?" but he was patronising me, the GP had already rang him with all her records. He kept telling me to calm down, and he couldn't have said a worse thing. I told him, "I tell you something, Doctor, I'm one of nine kids. When my mum died she didn't leave me any possessions. But she left me something all the money in the world doesn't buy, that's courage, and I've got loads of that!"

As I walked out of there, he said, "I'm so sorry about how things have worked out." I said, "No sorrier than me!" They may be professors, but they're doing a job the same as you or me. They're not infallible. Deana was let down by the National Health.

When I came home I rang my firm up and they told me to tell her to go private, that they would pay for it. But no. "Mum, I don't want no fuss." She wouldn't let them.

But I needed help, so I thought of Peter Hain, who was

now an MP. His mum and dad still used to send me Christmas cards till I moved from Belton Way. So I rang his secretary up – I don't know if she was the woman he ended up married to.

"I'm really shocked to hear that him and Pat," she'd been his wife, "are divorcing."

"If you don't mind me asking," she said, "where do you know Mr Hain from?"

"I went to Oxford with him!"

When I thought about it afterwards, I laughed. She must have heard my voice and thought, "How could *she* have been to Oxford?" What I have should have said was 'a seminar on the criminal justice system' in Oxford.

But of course he didn't phone back. He didn't want to know the likes of us anymore. He'd jumped on our campaign bandwagon but we'd outgrown our use.

So we moved Deana to Guy's Hospital. I knew she was really ill then. Through a friend of mine, I got an appointment with Dr Price at the London Clinic, so I was eventually able to put her in there. I didn't know where the money was going to come from, but I knew I'd get it somehow. As it turned out, as I worked for a bank I was able to get a loan from them. She really was special, and she had wonderful friends. I got cheques through my door for £1,000 at a time. How many friends would do that? Her dear friend Denise, who she was very close to, organised a benefit dance. You can't buy a friendship like that. And my friends were wonderful, I was able to borrow money off of them too. It cost forty grand in all, but I managed to scrape it all together.

Deana took it in her stride. Never moaned, never said she didn't feel well. But she didn't look well. Her looks really didn't pity her.

She wasn't with her partner from that point right up until the end. He was a good dad, I couldn't take that away from him, but he didn't work. So I felt responsible for her family as well. Rick was very good. He had a good job down the market and he looked after his sister.

RICK

We got through the period of my dad being in prison for the LEB thing together really. If my mum wasn't out working, she'd be on the campaign, doing things for my dad, visiting or whatever. So Deana was always there for me, cooking for me or looking after me. When I was a bit older and she moved out, she was only across the road. The pub where I drank was underneath her flat, so I was always around there or she was always around ours.

But at one point I was sitting there on a Saturday morning, after she'd had about four lots of chemo. The phone went.

"Mum, I'm up in the London Hospital. Nanny found Granddad on the floor this morning!"

George was away on holiday, in Lanzarotte I think. But instead of phoning the other son they'd rung Deana, who was ill. They'd put him on life support. She loved her granddad.

I said, "Come home here, we'll have a bit of breakfast Let them do all the tests and whatever."

She said, "No, I don't think he's gonna make it." And he didn't.

She was heartbroken. That kid sat up in that hospital till he died.

George didn't rush to get home. So my son and daughter made all the funeral arrangements because their nan was ill. George's brother did nothing.

My son is a little bit more outspoken than Deana, so he told my mother-in-law, "Nan, Uncle Ricky's not done a thing."

She said, "Well, he ain't used to . . ."

"We ain't used to it," he said, "but we've done it."

Because she was ill, my mother-in-law didn't want to stay in the flat on her own. So we all took it in turns. (George never stayed once, and yet it was his mum.) I used to finish work sometimes at eleven o'clock, but I'd stay a couple of nights a week.

I'd say to her, "I won't be home until about twelve."

"That's alright," she said.

As much as I loved my mother-in-law, I look back now and I think she was selfish. Maybe that's who George took after. Deana was ill, and Ann was aware of it, but she'd still let her go round there and clean.

George would go see her every day, but only for about ten minutes. All she really wanted was his time. I'd go round there to clean her windows, but he could have done that.

Deana would be there, cleaning. "Leave that!" I'd tell her. "I'll do that!" But she was such a good girl. Every day she'd go shopping for her nan. Perhaps that's what kept her going for a while.

When I was still working for the bank, Wendy Richard, who used to be on *Eastenders*, lived round the corner. It was in the news that she'd had breast cancer a while before.[1] I

---

1 *In early October 2008, an announcement was made to the press that Wendy Richard had suffered a relapse, the cancer spreading to her bones and internal organs. Due to her terminal condition, Ms Richard had made immediate plans to marry her partner, John Burns.*

don't know how I got talking to her, but I said that my daughter had been diagnosed.

When she was on a programme about breast cancer shortly after, she talked about how she'd recently met a lady whose daughter was suffering with it. When I saw her again, I said how nice it was of her to mention Deana – although it wasn't by name.

Deana had been through her chemotherapy, which shrunk the tumour. But even after all that she still had her breast removed. I remember going in when she had the operation, and this Swedish doctor said, "We don't like visitors." I thought, I am *not* going to stay away today, of all days!

Me and my son went up there at eleven o'clock at night. They had her covered in silver foil, she was sweating, she didn't know we were there. All these needles were hanging out of her neck. But she never made any fuss.

Whenever she saw the doctor it was still, "How have you been?" "Yeah, I'm fine," but I knew she wasn't. She was frightened to ask questions.

In the end, when she did start to complain, I took her away on holiday with some of her friends. She'd say, "Mum, I've had enough! I don't want to go back in the hospital." I'd say, "Now come on, don't give up!"

Poor little cow.

When we got home I took her to Harley Street. The cancer had gone to her liver by then. The consultant said, "We can perform a transplant," but I'd already found out from the internet that, because it was secondary, nothing could be done. If it had started in the liver, they could take so much of it away and she might have recuperated. But because it was secondary, *no*.

But what could I say? I couldn't sit there in front of her and say, "Oh no you can't!"

Deana was a good looking girl, and she liked a drop of wine too. I'd say, "You're as silly as nuts, you are! You let people take you on." "Mum, I can't be like you!" she'd say. She wasn't like me, she wasn't fiery, but she wasn't a fool. Deana would think things through before she spoke. Me, I'm out with it, and I know I haven't always been right.

She had friends all over – from little kids, who loved her, to a couple she met in New York when George's cousin took her there on holiday. They still write to me, they call us "our English family". If only Deana had lived to get to know them properly. But they only came over once before she died.

Rick's eldest one was only two when Deana died, and Deana loved her. I'd go up there and she'd have everyone in with their kids. I'd say, "All their places are nice and clean, look at yours." "Oh Mum, I don't care!" She always had a houseful and she let them do what they liked.

Deana left a lasting impression on everyone. (Someone once said I do too. For all the wrong reasons, I reckon.)

On the last day I went to see her in hospital, she said, "I'm just going to go in and have a wash." As she went in the bathroom, I said, "Close the door and I'll straighten your bed and that." The doctors were coming, and I didn't want her to see me talking to them.

They took me into the room and told me, "I'm afraid we've done all we can." Oh, what a terrible day.

The doctor said, "I told her father, and he walked away." I said, "Yeah, that sounds like him." Once again he couldn't face it.

But neither could I. I couldn't even go back in that room

– the nurse had to collect my bag out of there. I begged them, "Please don't tell her."

The next day, when I went in, Deana said, "Mum, where did you go?" I said, "I went down to pay some money and when I came back you were fast asleep." They'd given her an injection.

My son went up there after I'd left, but of course he wasn't told. I rang him on his mobile. "You'd better come straight from the hospital." He was heartbroken. I said, "Now we've got to make the most of whatever time she's got left."

Sometimes I change my mind about it, but I'd like to think that she never knew. I said to her, "Come home with me till you get your strength back." She told me, "I ain't going back there, Mum. I don't like it there." And she never left me. She stayed with me for the last six months of her life.

But I went back to the clinic. I told the doctor, "You gave us false hope." Which he did, but I could never have said it in front of her. He said to me, "I'll arrange for the hospice," but I said no, her GP would send a nurse in. As soon as she heard the word 'hospice' then she would have known. She wasn't stupid.

They sent in this Australian nurse called Rowena. She was a lovely girl, I called her 'Rowenta the iron'. She'd sit and have a coffee with me, and even after Deana died she came to see me. I asked her, "What do you think her life expectancy is?"

"It could be a month, it could be six weeks . . ."

So I made the best of what time we had. I had all her friends round, did all I could.

My mother-in-law, Ann, was in a home by this time. Deana was sat talking on my settee, and she said she wanted to visit her nan.

"With all those germs, you can't go and see Nan in there,"
I told her. "You can talk to her on the phone."

"I do miss her, Mum . . ."

"I know, but talk to her on the phone and once you get
your strength back, we'll think about it."

I said to one of my friends the other week, "The only thing
I regret is that I stopped her from going to see her nan."

But she said, "No. You never did. She wrapped herself up,
went and saw her anyway."

I thought, "The little cow! She went against what
I said." But it really did make me feel better, in a weird
sort of way. She only went a couple of times, I think,
unbeknownst to me.

(My mother-in-law died in the same year as Deana. I believe
she died of a broken heart. She was in a home by this point,
as she couldn't take care of herself. My daughter's youngest,
Lauren, came crying to me after that. "Nan, Granddad's only
going to let Nanny's funeral go from that home!" They loved
their great nan too – she was 'Nanny' to them. But I said no.
I had Ann's funeral leaving from my house, and we all went
to the pub for a few drinks – except George.)

I had to keep three big bottles of morphine in the fridge
for Deana. She'd say, "I'm going to have some morphine and
I'm going back to bed now." She used to hang onto the stairs
as she went up. I would follow her up but I didn't sleep. If
she called out it was like I was on a spring.

I used to have to lie through my teeth, because she didn't
realise how ill she was. I'd go round to the doctor's and say,
"I won't be a minute, I'm going round to the shop." All silly
little lies, but I used to hate it.

When she was lying ill I'd get on the train to work, going
all the way to Baker Street and sometimes going past my

stop because I was thinking about her. But her friends used to come round and look after her while I was at work.

George never had any of that, of course, though he did maintain contact through my son. I wouldn't allow him in, I'd say to Rick, "Tell him to go, get out!" Though I did let him in just once, before she died.

Deana died on the seventh of March 2001. She never left my house, love her. She'd always say, "I'd hate to lie in an undertaker's," and she didn't, she stayed here all the time.

When I made Deana all ready, laid her out and washed her, Rowena said, "How did you know how to do that?" I told her about my nan. "You could get yourself a job," she said.

No, thanks. But little did I know at the time that I'd use that knowledge all those years later.

Rick doesn't say a lot about it, but where she was seven years older she was like a little mum to him. He wasn't a big boy and if any kids started on him he'd say, "I'm going to get my sister," she'd come to the door and they'd all run.

He idolised her, loved her to bits. When she and her chap broke up when the kids were little, and she was struggling, he was a good boy to her. She used to say to me, "Mum, I'll go to the drawer and there's £40 he's put in there." He'd do it really discreetly.

But oh God, he misses her. He misses her now more than ever.

RICK

Everyone loved her. When she died they all came to the service, even my mates, all the lads from the pub. She was just a lovely, lovely girl. She was beautiful. Never had a bad word to say about anyone.

Deana should have had a better life than she did. She got mixed up with someone who didn't work, and she was so young when she had the kids. Alright, that was her choice. But I wish she'd have enjoyed herself more, though she wasn't one for going out.

She loved the kids and they were her life, but I look at other people and I think, "Oh, I wish she'd have done more." I wish I'd done more with my life too, but she had two kids, she was in a council place, at least she might have had a garden, a nicer environment. She really was a good mum though.

Even now, there's not a day that goes by when I don't think of her. It's like the song: "There's always something there to remind me." I go to a drawer, there's something in there that she bought me the last Christmas before she died. I put the radio on and the song that always reminds me of my daughter comes on, 'I Will Survive'. She always used to sing along to that, though she couldn't sing.

And when I finished work on a Friday, I used to go in John Lewis's to buy her something to cheer her up. I don't know how many Hoovers I bought my girl. She was terrible with electrical things. If I'd got a decent tip I'd buy her a new bed set. I can't go in John Lewis's now.

Christmas will never be the same. She loved it, she stacked all the presents up underneath the tree. I went to my son's last year, and he had his in-laws over, but they all miss her at Christmas. (Not that I liked Christmas anyway – but I suppose that stems from when we were kids, and we had nothing.) That last one that we had together, me and her stood at the door, following the old tradition of banging your pots and pans to see in the new and let out the old.

There she was with no hair, in her nightie and old socks. "If anyone walked by here now," I said, "they'd say, 'Look at those two fucking nutters!'"

On Christmas Day we had my son here with his wife, and Deana's two girls. (The younger one, Lauren, was eighteen when Deana died, and the eldest, Emma, was twenty-three.) She normally cooked Christmas dinner every year, she loved it, but now she couldn't eat anything. "Oh Mum, that smells lovely," she told me. I said, "Try and eat a little bit," but no. Rick had a video camera, but she said, "Don't put that camera on me! Next year you can." I thought, "*Oh, dear God . . .*"

You should have seen my street on the day of her funeral, it was covered in flowers. You couldn't have got another person in the church, even the priest said so, and the service was at the big church in the middle of the East India Dock Road. She had a good send-off – if you can call it 'good' when you're saying goodbye to one of your kids.

She never left my house till the day she was cremated. I still keep her ashes in the corner. They'll go when I go. I'd like to think we go to a better place. That was all that kept me going throughout the whole time.

I had a special urn made. I was going to bury her out in the garden, but then I thought, no, she didn't like the cold, I can't put her out there.

It's a funny thing but, when he was at work, George had a friend who worked in Hatton Garden, the jeweller's place. At the time big crosses were all the go. He had one made for me at Christmas, out of nine-carat gold.

Years later I offered it to George's cousin's son, who is a priest. My mum always used to say, "You carry three crosses in your life." I felt that, when I looked back over the years, I'd carried mine and a few other people's, so I wanted to get rid of it. I just felt it was a bad omen. But the priest didn't want it, so I tried to sell it. "For what they're offering you," I was told, "you'd sooner throw it away.

So I put it in Deana's hands, and that cross went with her.

How does that saying go? "Lord, grant me the serenity to accept the things I cannot change . . ."

10

AFTER DEANA

It always seemed to me that, as I got over one thing, then something else dramatic would happen. Three weeks after losing Deana, my eldest granddaughter, Emma, came in to tell me she was pregnant. I thought, "Oh, I don't believe it!"

She'd been courting her fellah for three years, so it was none of my business really. But there were only her and her sister living in my daughter's flat. I was thinking, "What's going to happen to the young one? She hasn't only lost her mum, she'll be losing her."

Which she did. But it made Lauren stronger. She was only eighteen, but she lived up at that flat on her own and it must have taken some courage.

It had been a happy home. Deana always had the records on, and they were more like sisters than mother and daughters.

I used to worry about Lauren. Thank God that she got out of there, and got a flat over on the Island. It's not a very nice area but it's a new flat, and it's a step on the ladder. She's got a good job so she can afford her own flat.

After I lost my own job, I worked as a housekeeper in a

children's hospice. Someone said to me at the time, "How can you do it?" These kids are terminally ill, but you'd be amazed by how much satisfaction, how much of a reward, you get from working with them.

But the staff nurse was one of those that always patronises you. I took it for a little while, but she had that air that says, *"I'm better than you."*

No one's better than me. Everyone's my equal. I have served some posh people, and I talk to them like I'm talking to you. I won't put on airs and graces. You'd only slip up, wouldn't you? But I know how to address people and I know when to joke about.

We knew we were having a meeting on a particular day, and we all had to contribute to it. It was to get feedback as to how the place was running, and how happy you were there. So there were the nursing staff, the housekeepers and the cook. The cook said, "You wait, I'm going to get up there tomorrow and tell her she's too bossy. I'm gonna tell her this, I'm gonna tell her that." The meeting went ahead, they got round to him and asked, "Have you got anything to contribute to the meeting?" "Nah, not really!" I looked at him and thought, am I going funny? "Anyway, I've got to go, I've got a stew on." Up he got and walked out of the meeting. Then it was my turn. "Have you got anything to contribute?" "Yeah, I've got quite a lot," I said." I had to put the staff nurse straight in the end. "I find you very patronising. You always talk down to people. Well it stops here!"

They all sat there with their mouths open. I think a lot of them would like to have said it but none of them had the guts. I could see the staff nurse going red, because the head of care was there.

I wouldn't be there that long anyway.

I've had a total of five lumps removed over a period of thirty years, and the first four were all what are called calcification lumps. But then, finally, I think that everything I thought had passed me by over the years started to come out in me.

On the last one, the fifth tumour, the consultant said to me, "We're going to leave this one," because all the others had been benign.

I said, "You ain't!" As you know, I've always been a little bit militant.

Him and the nurse looked over at me. "You can't speak to Mr So-and-so like that!" she told me.

I said, "If I had two grand to put in his hand, he'd soon have it out."

I jumped up off the trolley, got dressed and came home. Two hours later there was a knock at the door. There was a porter standing there with a letter. They had put me in the private ward, all because I'd spoken up.

Then, in March 2004, I had a bad fall. I fell down on the pavement, and as I did I felt the whole of my insides turn over from the tips of my toes.

I'd fractured my arm so I went to the hospital. I managed to go away on holiday after that with some of Deana's friends, but then I found another lump. When I went back to the doctor she sent me to Bart's.

I had to have all the tests and I was diagnosed in one day. Of course, they said it was breast cancer.

I didn't mess about. "They're coming off!"

But they don't like to do that. "We'll just do a . . ."

"No, they're coming off!" They always have a nurse there in case you become hysterical. I said to her, "I don't want a lot of fuss. But it's got to be done."

I knew too much about breast cancer because of Deana. With hindsight I wish I hadn't known anything.

I said to them, "I don't want to hang around. I want to get in and get it done." So they did it. I was in there within three weeks.

That October, I came back from staying with my friend Pauline in Spain. It was Deana's birthday, when I always go to Westminster Cathedral to light a candle. Pauline came with me. On one arm I had a little gnat bite, but this arm kept getting redder and redder.

After leaving the cathedral, I thought I'd better go round to the doctor's. They sent me up to the London Hospital where they kept me in. I had cellulitis – which is dangerous, it poisons your blood – and blood clots. Then I got it in the leg. And then, when I had a scan, that's when they found that the cancer had spread.

Of course they try to pussyfoot around you. I didn't ask a lot of questions, but it's hard to take it in. You think, "I'm dreaming this."

One of the doctors told me, "Your reputation precedes you." I won't put up with any bullshit. I was having the strongest chemotherapy you can have at first, and I said to Dr Maier, who's in charge, "I don't mind, but I want you to be honest. I don't wanna be a guinea pig for pharmaceutical companies." He gave me such a look.

I didn't begrudge it to Deana, but I wouldn't pay for private doctors now. You get a lovely room, you get all the attention, you get lovely food. But you don't get any better treatment. The only advantage is that you get seen quicker.

Looking back now, if I'd have let that fifth tumour go I'd have been in the position I am now a few years earlier.

I think it's God's way of telling me I've got to slow down. I'd have never sat as long in a chair as I have to now. The hardest thing for me is asking anyone to do something for me. I've had to eat humble pie.

I went to the hospital with my old friend, Hetty, who comes with me. I couldn't wish for lovelier neighbours than in my street. But then they're the old school. My little street is like going back in time. Everyone knows everyone and everyone would help one another. But those days are gradually going. People are moving away or dying, and you're getting the youngsters in.

The nurse tried to insert a needle into me in three places. At first I thought, "Be patient," but in the end I was going, "No, leave it! You're just making me bruised. Go and get someone that can do it!"

The sister came and did it right away. The nurse had spent hours messing about. Imagine someone sticking a needle in you for that long. My tolerance is now literally zero, and I never thought I'd get like that. I get irritable lining up anywhere, I want to be there first. It's terrible, but perhaps my patience will come back.

I sincerely doubt it though.

But then I looked at some of the people at the hospital, and I thought, "What am I moaning for?" These were really ill people.

"But *you're* really ill," Hetty said to me.

"Yeah, but I ain't laid up, I can still get around."

Then she went and got me a wheelchair. I said, "Are you taking the piss? I've got a stick 'ere."

But I did get in it, I've got to be honest. She's eighty-odd and she was wheeling me about. My legs felt terrible.

But when people say, "You *are* brave," I don't think I'm

brave at all. We're all going to die one day – be it today, tomorrow or whenever.

I've had my debts in the past and wondered where the next bit of money was coming from – especially when my girl was ill and I had to put her in the hospital. That very year she died, I was made redundant, but eventually I cleared all my debts.

I've come to a time in my life when I've got no money worries; I've got friends who live abroad who I could go to see whenever I wanted to. I should be on top of the world. And now this happens. What's the good of money if you haven't got your health?

But at least I've had a life. I thank my lucky stars when I wake up every morning. How many people go out of their door, say, "Bye, see you later," and never come home again? They haven't had time to make any arrangements. There are young kids out there dying of cancer too. I think I'm fortunate in a lot of respects.

Life can be cruel, but you just have to get on with it. I've often had people say to me, " I don't know how you cope." Well, what else can you do?

What else can you do?

I've got a friend who's nursed her husband for thirteen years. They were the loveliest couple. He was a captain on the pleasure boats, but then he got a brain tumour. It changed her life. At least when I'm alright I can go wherever I like. She can't walk out the door, it's like leaving a baby. It breaks my heart. They had everything, but they've got nothing left really.

And then, when I think of people like Jane Tomlinson, who kept going for nearly ten years and ran all those marathons before she died, I think that the mind is a

228

powerful tool. An awful lot can be overcome by thinking positively, as I try to do.

But I always think that what will be will be. No one can cheat it, however much money they've got. And I sometimes wish that it had been me that had gone instead of Deana. She's got two lovely grandchildren who she would have worshipped. Still, it wasn't to be.

People look at me sometimes and I can tell they're thinking, "Oh, you're hard!" Not that I give a shit what anyone thinks, to be quite honest. But I could have sat back many a time and felt sorry for myself. I could have had people doing everything for me.

But I'm not that type. I've always been independent and I find it hard to ask anyone to do anything for me, even now. My boy says, "Mum, you're *too* bleeding independent," but I can't help it. It's the way I am.

I had to laugh after the last time I got home from hospital. I'd never had a fag the whole time I was in there. He came in and went, "Oh Mum!", waving all my smoke away. I said, "I'm in my own home! Don't tell me what to do in my own home!"

I've got nothing to reproach myself for as a mother. I've no regrets whatsoever. I might have come across as tough with them at times, but then if I hadn't I'd have been walked over.

He's a good boy. Even when I don't feel well, I don't tell him about it. It wouldn't be fair, he drives a taxi for a living and he doesn't need a lot of distractions on his mind.

The nice thing about it is he can choose how many hours he wants to work. But I say to him, "Son, don't get like me." If I used to be offered two or three jobs, I'd take all three of them if I thought it would buy everything we needed. And then you look around and your life's gone. Where are all those years? If I had my life over again, I'd do a lot of things differently. (But then it's easy to say that, isn't it?)

Rick often tells me to come over during the week. Sometimes I have to tell him, "When I'm like this, I don't like being around the kids." You think children don't take notice, but they do. I don't want them thinking Nanny was always ill.

When I was ill for the first time I was convalescing at Lovistone, which is a beautiful place. I was up in my room and the phone rang.

"Your brother Colin's here."

My brother Colin? I hadn't seen him for a few years. I'd washed my hands of him too. It wasn't so much anything to do with my mum (he was the apple of her eye), as that he walked out on my sister-in-law and her three boys for another woman one Christmas. It broke all of their hearts.

I was close to him, but now all those years had elapsed. It was sad really.

As I came downstairs he walked towards me with a great big bouquet of flowers. That woman stood behind him. I said, "I think you've got a fucking nerve coming 'ere!"

Everything was a laugh to him. He had a lovely personality. We went out and had a coffee after that, but I couldn't make conversation with that woman. I wasn't rude to her but I didn't make her too welcome. It would have been disloyal to my sister-in-law.

I said ta-ta to him, and I never saw him anymore until I heard he was really ill. My sister-in-law told me that he had prostate cancer, but on principle I really couldn't go and see him.

But then this is how strange people can be. My sister-in-law rang me to say she'd been down there the week before, and this woman had cooked them dinner.

"You sat at her table?" I couldn't believe it. "On principle, Jean, I've kept away for years and you're sitting there eating her dinner?"

"Well, it happened years ago!"

"What would you have said if I'd made myself busy, gone down to where he lives and had a drink with them?" I think I took her breath away. Sometimes I wish I could bend, but I just can't help the way I am.

"Sometimes you just have to let things go," she said.

I told her, "No, Jean, you don't, not in my book. I can't put it at the back of my mind and forget about it."

And then I thought, why? He was really ill, after all. My Rick wanted to go and see him; he loved Colin.

We went on the Saturday, and he died on the Sunday. I'm glad that I went now. He was pleased to see me; his eldest boy, David, was there too. (He actually named his first daughter after me. Poor little cow!) I'm glad Jean was honest with me, because I would have been more than upset to think I hadn't gone to see him.

I don't see any of my family now. I lost all contact down to Colin and my mum. When my niece was twenty-one she invited all of us to a big party in a hall. She said, "I don't care who's talking and who's not." I went to it, and my sister Doreen, who's since died, tried to make amends. She told me, "This is silly," and bought me a drink, but I still couldn't bend.

I met my sister Brenda coming home from work only a few years ago, when Deana was still here. She was going from Whitechapel to Bethnal Green, but I was getting off at the next stop. She asked me, "Did you know that Dickie's very ill?" He was our eldest brother.

"Yeah, so is my daughter."

"I did hear," she said. I've never spoken to her since. Brenda was at my daughter's funeral but she never came to my home, she stood at the end of the street.

I never went to my other brother's funerals, and I never went to my sister's. Brenda was at Colin's funeral, but once again she never came back for a drink or anything. It's sad really, when you think of how a big family like ours has broken up. I envy families that are close.

But then my youngest brother came up to me at the funeral and I told him to fuck off. I couldn't help it. He said, "What have I done?" and he walked away. I'd spoken to him when Deana was ill, because he was upset and he came to see her. But ever since I'd been ill I'd not heard from him.

Peter Chappell broke his heart at that funeral. I look at him now and he's an old man, but he was such a big, strapping bloke back then. We'd just seen Colin on the video, and we'd just buried him, but to see a man cry like that is hard.

Mickey Ishmail is not long gone too. After him and Jeannie split up, I can't remember the last time I saw him. He died in France in 2004, on holiday with Terry Calvey. My son told me when I was in hospital, when I was ill the first time. That was drug-related. Terry liked a drink, but Mickey liked a drug.

His eldest daughter was at my granddaughter's wedding because she was Deana's friend. She said that they lost his body coming back through France. No one knew where he was. I know I shouldn't laugh, but I did. Still, if I'd been around when he was being buried I'd have definitely gone to his funeral.

PETER

I think Ishmail ended up dealing in drugs. But even that was small-time compared to the others. He was on the coke. There are people around here of my age stuffing it up their noses. They can't do without it. You go in the local pub and they're always standing by the toilets, they're in and out all fucking night. They're supposed to be villains, living off their fucking glory. They've done fuck-all for forty years!

George was at Colin's funeral. You wouldn't know he was the same man. Lost his hair. Got a great big beer gut. I think he had a cheek even going, to be honest. He never showed respect to Colin when he was here, so why show it when he's dead?

When I came out of the crematorium, Peter was talking to George who was there on his own. Peter had never met my Colin's David, so I called him over. I completely ignored George. Another man might have turned around and walked away, but he just stood there.

My granddaughter got married last year, it was a beautiful wedding. I booked a little Holiday Inn for us to stay in. He was there with his wife. She's a nice girl, but I look at her and think, "Oh you silly cow!" He wouldn't have spoken to me in the way he talks down to her.

They were both sitting there having breakfast as I walked in.

"Morning Jenny!"

"Morning Rose!"

"Wasn't the wedding nice?"

"Did you enjoy it?"

He was just sitting there, tucking in. She's very polite but he's wary of me, stays right out of my way. He would rather die than confront me. (What is he frightened of *me* for, given the size of me?)

I know he's there but I can look right through him.

George sees Deana's girls at parties, but he doesn't ring them up. He calls my boy every day, but not the rest of them. I think his father keeps more in touch with him than it would be if it were the other way round, if you know what I mean.

RICK

Me and my dad are alright. I spoke to him this morning. I've been on holiday with him, I go out drinking with him – not so much now that I've got a family, but he comes round to my house. I get on alright with Jenny too, she's as good as gold really.

David Whitehouse, the QC, approached him about taking his case to the Court of Appeal.[1] Dad wants to bring it to a conclusion, to draw a line under it, and finally get his name cleared for the LEB. There was always forensic evidence, but nowadays it would be laughed straight out of court, it's so easy to test it.

I think what irks him is he's a driver now, and the Public Carriage Office wouldn't give him a full cab driver's licence. Because of the work he was doing he was carrying children about, and they said that because of his criminal record he wasn't allowed to.

Well, he's not a fucking nonce! Yet Ruth Kelly could let

---

1 *In early 2007, it was announced that David Whitehouse QC was taking George Davis's appeal for a full overturning of his conviction to the Criminal Cases Review Commission (CCRC). The case is ongoing.*

fucking paedophiles work in schools.[2] *How does that work out? But because he was an armed robber he couldn't take disabled children to school.*

Anyway, he's now appealed against his 1975 conviction, but I think it was Whitehouse who got the ball rolling. My dad said to me, "I get the feeling that he likes me and that he just wants to do it."

GEORGE

I hope we can get back to the appeal court and actually get the conviction quashed, because it would vindicate me. I could say to all of the people in the campaign, "You were right – I didn't do it."

I haven't heard any more for a few months because David Whitehouse has been busy. I'm just waiting for the CCRC to come back and confirm whether they accept it. It's good to have a QC who can actually put a legal case together now. I was so pleased that he picked it up.

We've started perfecting grounds. David has made a good, strong argument on paper, especially as we're going back to the blood evidence. That should never have allowed it to go to trial, let alone to a conviction.

Have they got stuff with DNA on? This is obviously one of the vital pieces of evidence. What about the photographs of the guy's profile? The guy that they always said was me,

---

2 *In 2006, during Ruth Kelly's tenure as Secretary of State for Education and Skills, it emerged that a man cautioned by police for viewing child pornography had been allowed to work at a school, despite inclusion on the national Sex Offenders Register. One of Ms Kelly's departmental ministers took responsibility, but it was then revealed that an offender convicted of the indecent assault of a fifteen-year-old girl was also cleared to work as a teacher.*

in the flying helmet, didn't look as tall as me. Is there a
possibility that they could tell how tall he was using the
new technology?

John Marriage was the QC and David Whitehouse was still
junior counsel back then. John was a lovely man, but he's
dead now. I've been sent letters from David. They keep
harassing me to give an interview.

No. Why should I put myself out now?

There's an old fellah I see even now. I won't mention his
name, but he's an old man. Back then he was well known. I
went in a coach with him to a nightclub that he was
running. Jeannie Ishmail came with me that night. I told her
to keep her mouth shut and mind her own business. It took
a lot to shut her up.

And I asked if it was him that had grassed them up,[3]
because that is what I'd heard. He went as white as a sheet,
and he said, "I admire you for your courage because no man
would ever say that to me. If you were a man I'd kill you
stone dead."

He was quite a nice man, but still a bad man. At that time,
to call someone a grass was the worst thing anyone could
have said. I knew what sort of family he came from and I'd
known him for years. I just had to satisfy my own mind after
what I'd overheard in a pub.

I know who did the robbery now, but I would never say.
It's water under the bridge, and it wouldn't make any
difference. It was no one we knew though.

It was a policeman who told me, believe it or not. But then

---

3 *Rose effectively means 'fitted up'. As George emphasises, you cannot be*
'grassed up' for a crime you did not commit.

someone else, whose credibility I wouldn't question, came up with the same name.

I don't know how these people live with themselves. How could you do something and watch someone else go down for it?

But then people do, don't they?

I think the clever ones are those that keep it shut and don't stand around in pubs. Not that I'm glorifying thieving, but I think the ones that work on their own are the brainiest.

So George is trying to prove his innocence now? Well, he's thirty-two fucking years late! Why is he trying to prove it *now*? He should have done it when he had a wife and kids.

If he's trying to get compensation then if anyone wants compensating, I certainly do. So does Peter.

GEORGE

Quite frankly, I'd want to know why he never looked after my old woman. He knew he'd done it. They weren't plums, they were professional robbers – you could tell that by the way they hijacked the cars and so forth. They went to work, those boys, they were grafters. He didn't even have to make himself known, he could just have put some money through the letterbox. Didn't do it.

So as far as I'm concerned, I don't want him to go to prison but I couldn't give a fuck about him. Because my kids went without me and their mother was ill with lumps in her breast. She was trying to work and trying to keep the home together. That prick was walking around and he couldn't put a pound note in the door? No.

RICK

I used to get silly people say to me, "Your dad's George Davis?!" I'd say, "So what? He was fucking nothing and he got twenty years." I just think, "fuck off" when I hear dopey people like that.

My dad is my dad, and at the end of the day I love him. But I'd rather it not have happened. But then they're the sort who must look up to silly people like the Krays. It's the myth of all these East End gangsters, and the idea that Dad was somehow one of the line.

PETER

It's a tragedy what's happened to Rosie really. In some ways it'd have been better for her and her family if I hadn't known them, if that campaign hadn't taken place. He'd have done his fucking bird or maybe he'd have got out.

GEORGE

I was very fortunate; I had good friends like Peter; I had a good wife; I had a good family – not only my family, but Rose's family were all there for me. I don't think many other people would be that fortunate. Perhaps I'm giving myself a gee, but I think I must have been pretty well liked.

They had such a driving force in Peter, and what can you say about Rose? She was dying and she was still doing the campaign. Her brothers and all the old people in my family were prepared to lay down in the road, along with my friends' daughters and their kids; my cousin's husband, Richie, went to prison with Peter.

Those people were just brilliant, like Colin and Jimmy, God rest their souls. There were many others who I didn't even know, like the American girl, Geri. I don't think we

ever spoke two words to one another, but she wouldn't take
bail unless they gave it to the others. They put themselves in
jeopardy and they went to prison.

I've got to be quite frank: I really don't think I would
have had the courage to do it. I don't think I could actually
have put myself on the line like those people did.

Peter Chappell left his Christmas dinner with Shirley and
went up and did the Christmas tree lights. What a man he
is: "I know that man ain't done it, I'm not going to allow
him to go to prison." That was Peter.

Rose sat outside in a freezing cold van for a Christmas
vigil. Where did they get it all from? I'd probably have said,
"Yeah, I'll wait round the corner by a fire, or in the pub."
I must say they had much more courage than me. Much
more courage.

I always said that I wasn't wanted, right from the off. You
can't tell me that my mum was going in for an *eleventh*
child? And then I was born at number thirteen – you know
my thing about numbers by now.

I suppose there are things we would all like to change. But
I didn't want much out of life really, just to be happy. I didn't
want a house in the country, I wasn't asking for a lot. And
those early years with George weren't all bad, not at all. But
I often wonder if things might have been different.

I remember years ago, when Deana was little, before we
had Rick or I lost the other baby. I said to George, "I'd love
to emigrate to Canada."

At the time people were emigrating and making a new life
for themselves. Maybe I was looking for something more.
Canada sounded nice, and it's very cold there. (I like the
cold. I think you get more settled in the cold.)

"I'm not leaving my family," said George. He didn't take any chances back then. Yet he certainly took chances later.

But I would have emigrated all those years back. Who knows how things might have turned out? (There again, my brother who I've just buried emigrated to Australia for two years, and he hated it.)

It's funny how your life takes all these different paths. They say you make you own luck in life, so I really don't know where I went wrong.

It always seemed that, once I got over one thing, I only got a few months' grace before something else would happen. And they weren't little things either.

AFTERWORD

I've enjoyed life.

I've got wonderful friends who I'm thankful for. True friends, the type of people who stick by you when you're ill. Some people can't face certain things, but I'm very lucky.

I fell out of touch with my friend Pauline Clarke and her husband years ago, but she got back in contact when she heard Deana was ill. Her family have been like angels to me. Their son Steve has a heart of gold. If I won the lottery tomorrow I could never repay that boy.

They're all so very close, not like my family were, but then I wonder if that was because of the era I was brought up in. I tell my grandchildren, "We'd all sit down to dinner but you weren't allowed to talk at the table." Now they encourage you to talk, which is right as it's the only time you all get together.

All I've ever really wanted is to see my kids happy, and I think I've achieved that via my grandchildren.

My Rick has got a family now, and they live out in Brentwood. He's really done a lot to their place, he's worked bloody hard. He's so soppy with his kids, he's bought them a rabbit that they put on a lead and take for a walk. ("You're a silly idiot," I told him.)

They have good schools out there, it's a lovely place to bring kids up. Rick doesn't want his wife, Tracey, to work so that she can be there for them. He's seen how hard I worked because I used to take him out with me. I've told him, "I wish your father would have had that attitude." Tracey is a lovely girl and a good mum, and they're very, very happy.

When Rick turned forty, I paid for him to go to Vegas for a holiday, and I looked after his two little daughters. I used to pick them up from school, we'd have dinner and then it was, "What are we going to do tonight, Nan?" One night I took them to the pictures, another night swimming. Then I said, "We're doing spelling tonight." It was all silly little words, and one of them was 'shout'. The oldest one said, "You've forgotten something, Nan." I said, "What have I forgotten?" "The exclamation mark!" She was seven years old at the time. Her English is absolutely beautiful. Yet the younger one is all hands, she's good with her hands.

You've got to give kids a good education these days, you really have got to. Whereas years ago, if you were a girl, all your mum wanted was for you to get married and have kids of your own, so it wasn't so important.

My oldest granddaughter Emma's chap had a private education and his mum and dad are quite wealthy. Emma and Spencer have just moved into a new house in Chafford Hundred, in Essex. She's got a very responsible job, she works fulltime and she's got two kids. She works bloody hard, but she's got a lovely way with her.

My little great grandson, Archie, goes to a good school and he speaks with a plum in his mouth. He's six years old, and he talks so beautifully I'm frightened to speak to him. He rang me up the other evening: "Hello Nanny, how are you?"

"I'm feeling a lot better, thank you, Archie."

"I've got my own phone now. Daddy bought me my own mobile."

I said, "Your dad ought to be ashamed of himself!"

(Afterwards, I thought I'll ring him back: "Hello, it's Archie Gale here and I'm on my own phone." I pissed myself laughing!)

My daughter's younger one, Lauren, has got a good bit of spark in her. She doesn't suffer fools gladly. (The other one's the complete opposite. Providing her life's not being interfered with, she'll just carry on happily.) She's doing a surveyor's course, she's clever, just like her sister. "Ooh, our cat's got big balls!" I said to her, which made her laugh.

She looks at me and she reckons she knows what I'm thinking, that one. I've never wanted to be an encumbrance on any of them, but she drives me mad at times: "Nan, are you alright? Nan, I'm coming over!" She's her mother all over, though not to look at. She's a giver.

That's all my daughter really wanted, for them to be happy. I just wish she'd have lived to see it. But it wasn't to be.

For years, Peter Chappell has been saying to me that I should write a book. I said, "No, what's the point?" There's a big point now that I'm ill. I want to leave my kids something to remember me by in the future.

All the experiences I've had have made me wiser. A lot wiser. I was the sort of person who never looked for the bad in anyone. Now I can see things that I never would have seen before.

George could have written his own book years ago. But then, how would he justify what he did – not only to me, not even to his kids, but to the public? And besides, I think the women in this country have got more backbone than the men.

Now, I just want to carry on with what life I've got left. As long as my kids are happy, so am I.

My troubles have all gone away now.